YEARS A, B, AND C

# Hopeful
*Meditations*

*for*
*Every Day*
*of Easter*
*Through*
*Pentecost*

*Rev. Warren J. Savage*

*Mary Ann McSweeny*

D1449774

Liguori
ONE LIGUORI DRIVE
LIGUORI MO 63057-9999

Imprimi Potest:
Harry Grile, CSsR, Provincial
Denver Province, The Redemptorists

Published by Liguori Publications
Liguori, Missouri 63057

To order, call 800-325-9521
www.liguori.org

**Library of Congress Cataloging-in-Publication Data**
Savage, Warren J.
    Hopeful meditations for every day of Easter through Pentecost
years A, B, and C / by Warren J. Savage and Mary Ann McSweeny.
        p. cm.
    ISBN 978-0-7648-2141-7 (pISBN) — ISBN 9780764822971E (eISBN)
    1. Eastertide—Prayers and devotions.  2. Pentecost—Prayers and
devotions.  3. Church year—Prayers and devotions.  4. Catholic Church.
Lectionary for Mass (U.S.)  I. McSweeny, Mary Ann. II. Title.
    BV55.S317 2013
    242'.36—dc23
                                                    2012041786

Liguori Publications, a nonprofit corporation, is an apostolate of
The Redemptorists. To learn more about The Redemptorists, visit
Redemptorists.com.

Printed in the United States of America
17 16 15 14 13 / 5 4 3 2 1
First Edition

# Contents

# Introduction

Jesus Christ is risen! The message of the resurrection is good news for the whole world. Life triumphs over death. Love triumphs over hatred. Hope triumphs over despair. Peace triumphs over conflict. Through the death and resurrection of Jesus, all of creation has been transformed and renewed. We believe that the resurrection event released us from the bondage of the world, setting us free to be with God in a new reality. Our lives are now interpreted through the lens of the resurrection.

The Easter Proclamation tells us that Christ is "the one Morning Star who never sets." Jesus is the eternal light that shines love and peace on all humanity. We have this eternal light in our hearts. We are called to live in this light and to be this light in a dark, chaotic, and fearful world. We have the power to change the world and to lead others to God. What we need is the courage to be people of the resurrection.

The Easter season is a time of hope and inner spiritual renewal. It is a graced period in which we can reflect on the meaning of the resurrection, deepen our relationship with the risen Lord, and intensify our efforts to bring the fruits of the resurrection—love, compassion, joy, peace, and forgiveness—to others. We need the Easter season to strengthen our hearts and our resolve to follow in the footsteps of the risen Lord.

The resurrection of Jesus affirms God's promise to be with us always, to love us unconditionally, to give us eternal life, joy, and peace. It is now time for us to reaffirm our promise to live with God, to be children of the light, and to renounce the empty promises of the world. The resurrection is a wonderful gift to the world and all humanity. Our challenge is to be this gift and share this gift with believers and unbelievers alike.

These hopeful meditations, inspired by the Scriptures, offer Christian pilgrims spiritual nourishment for the journey during the Easter season. By reading, reflecting on, and praying with the Word of God, we are strengthened, transformed, and enlightened by the Spirit of God to be humble witnesses to the presence of the risen Lord in our lives.

# Easter Season

# Monday of the Octave of Easter

*Acts 2:14, 22–33*
*Psalm 16:1–2a and 5, 7–8, 9–10, 11*
*Matthew 28:8–15*

**So they left the tomb quickly with fear and great joy, and ran to tell his disciples. Suddenly Jesus met them and said, "Greetings!" And they came to him, took hold of his feet, and worshiped him. Then Jesus said to them, "Do not be afraid; go and tell my brothers to go to Galilee; there they will see me."**

**MATTHEW 28:8–10**

*Reflection:* Our imagination is a powerful tool to find meaning in the gospels. Our imagination allows us to become part of this story. We can see ourselves going to the tomb of Jesus, and once we arrive, something incredible happens. A messenger appears and tells us that Jesus is raised from the dead. The messenger tells us to go and tell the disciples, but on the way we encounter the risen Jesus. Our first instinct is to embrace him with deep love, reverence, and respect. Jesus then instructs us to go and tell his brothers the good news: that he is alive.

Our imagination allows us to experience the joy and excitement surrounding the resurrection of Jesus. Our imagination also opens up a way for us to understand what it means to be a Christian witness in the world today. When we prayerfully read the Word of God, take time to appreciate the beauty of creation, show respect for others, and respond to people's needs, the resurrection becomes real in our lives. The story of the resurrection makes us eager to tell others about our experience of the risen Lord in our lives.

Perhaps we have mixed feelings about our faith. Perhaps telling others about the risen Jesus fills us with fear and great joy. We do not have to be afraid. With the help of the Holy Spirit and empowered by the resurrection of Jesus, we can be God's messengers of hope, compassion, peace, and reconciliation.

*Ponder:* Why am I afraid to share my faith with others?

*Prayer:* Risen Lord, your life-giving presence gives me hope, strength, and peace. Help me to be your witness of love and compassion in the presence of others.

*Practice:* Today I will look at people and greet them with respect and reverence.

# Tuesday of the Octave of Easter

*Acts 2:36–41*
*Psalm 33:4–5, 18–19, 20 and 22*
*John 20:11–18*

**Mary Magdalene went and announced to the disciples, "I have seen the Lord."**

JOHN 20:18

*Reflection:* From grief to joy, from despair to hope, from turmoil to peace, from loneliness to feeling loved. When we recognize the resurrected Jesus, we are transformed. Our very lives carry a message of love, peace, hope, and joy to others.

Before we reach this state of transformation, however, we spend a lot of time searching for our meaning and purpose, for support and encouragement, for the assurance that we are loved and needed. We often tend to search outside ourselves: at work, in our faith community, in our support groups, with our friends and relatives. Yet the real search happens inside the tomb of our inner self. Inside this tomb we have buried our innate wisdom, our intimate knowledge of God, our sense of self-worth, and our power to love and heal others and ourselves.

Our inner truth is often buried beneath layers of habitual mindsets and behaviors that drain us of positive energy: needing to be in control, wanting to be perfect, being disdainful and suspicious of those who are different, being afraid to speak out against injustice and violence, holding on to our possessions instead of sharing them with those in need.

Sifting through the debris in our innermost tombs is an adventure to which God calls us every day. We are called to know our true nature as children of God, to feel God's love in our lives and hearts, and to accept that God made us in love, for love. We are called to empty our tombs so that we have space for God to fill us with the gifts of hope, joy, peace, and love. Then our lives will announce God's goodness and kindness in the world.

*Ponder:* What do I need to clear out of my tomb?

*Prayer:* Risen Lord, you are my help and my hope. Give me the courage to empty myself of all that prevents me from knowing your goodness and kindness.

*Practice:* Today I will clean out a cluttered area of my home.

# Wednesday of the Octave of Easter

*Acts 3:1–10*
*Psalm 105:1–2, 3–4, 6–7, 8–9*
*Luke 24:13–35*

**But Peter said, "I have no silver or gold, but what I have I give you; in the name of Jesus Christ of Nazareth, stand up and walk."**

**ACTS 3:6**

*Reflection:* Most of us think that if we had lots of money, we'd be freer, more powerful, more able to help in the world. We imagine all the good we could do if we were to win the lottery. We'd give a big donation to the Church, pay off someone's loans, or take the time to relax and enjoy life. We live in a state of delusion and frustrated expectation because we have put our hope in money instead of in God.

God is more powerful than money. And so are we. Without any silver or gold, Peter heals the man who was lame by aligning his own power of compassion with the healing power of Jesus. We don't need money to let our power of love and faith transform the world. We just need to use what we already have to help others experience the love and healing forgiveness of God.

Maybe we have the gift of hospitality. We can heal the wound of loneliness by inviting others to sit at our table.

Maybe we have the gift of patience. We can heal the wound of discouragement by staying positive even in the face of pain, illness, and adversity.

Maybe we have the gift of laughter. We can heal the wound of bitterness by finding the humor in the events of our daily lives.

God asks each of us to give what we have in the moment. God asks us to rejoice in our gifts and talents and to use them to serve others. God asks us to trust more in God's power of love than in silver or gold.

*Ponder:* What do I have to give to others?

*Prayer:* Risen Lord, you are glorious and good. Help me to seek the transforming power of your love and forgiveness.

*Practice:* Today I will make a list of the gifts I have and use one of them to help someone in need.

# Thursday of the Octave of Easter

*Acts 3:11–26*
*Psalm 8:2ab and 5, 6–7, 8–9*
*Luke 24:35–48*

**While in their joy they were disbelieving and still wondering, [Jesus] said to them, "Have you anything here to eat?" They gave him a piece of broiled fish, and he took it and ate in their presence.**

LUKE 24:41–43

*Reflection:* Simple joy can be found in sharing food with others. Eating is essential to the human condition. Food is vital to our health.

Some people love food and have easy access to it. They love the flavors and textures food provides. They love fresh-baked bread, cookies, and pastries. They love meat, fish, fruit, vegetables, and exotic foods. They love sampling dishes from other parts of the world. They love the way food makes them feel. They love the joy and excitement associated with eating good food.

Some people love food but can't afford to buy enough of it. Some feel ashamed of being hungry. Some don't ask for help for fear of being judged or rejected. In a society of plenty, some people have difficulty getting enough to eat. They don't have the opportunity to experience the simple joy of eating with others.

In a world of abundant food, thousands of people are starving. Starvation means muscles are atrophying, bones are becoming desiccated, systems are shutting down, the brain is struggling to function, and death is painfully encroaching. Starvation happens because those with an abundance of food do not share with those who don't have enough. Greed and indifference are effectively killing millions of God's children.

Fed by God's Word, we are compelled to share our food with our brothers and sisters who do not have enough to eat. We give hope to the poor when we do all we can to eradicate hunger in our world.

*Ponder:* What does food and eating mean to me?

*Prayer:* Risen Lord, you know our human needs. Show me how to feed my sisters and brothers who have no food.

*Practice:* Today I will donate food to an organization that will distribute it to those who are starving.

# Friday of the Octave of Easter

*Acts 4:1–12*
*Psalm 118:1–2 and 4, 22–24, 25–27a*
*John 21:1–14*

**When they had gone ashore, they saw a charcoal fire there, with fish on it, and bread.**

JOHN 21:9

*Reflection:* Jesus has a welcoming fire going and a meal cooking for the hungry, hard-working fishermen. He knows his followers need comfort, attention, a good meal, fellowship, and a chance to relax in the presence of God. Jesus has a gift for intimacy. He cherishes every opportunity to spend time with people, getting to know them, listening to their problems, enjoying their companionship, finding ways to touch their hearts, giving them the chance to grow closer to him.

As we grow in the likeness of God, we learn to search out occasions for intimacy with others. We take notice of the people around us and offer them encouragement. We look for ways to ease others' burdens. We take the time to learn about others' likes and dislikes, strengths and weaknesses, hopes and dreams. We share our own experiences and problems, trusting others with a glimpse of our human vulnerability. We make opportunities to call, write, or visit. We let others know we care about them. We give hope to others when we reassure them that they are not alone.

As we spend time in intimate connection with others, we learn more about ourselves. We discover our levels of intolerance. We notice how difficult it is to listen without interrupting. We practice patience, nonjudgment, kindness, forgiveness, and compassion. We let go of our rigid sense of right and wrong. We learn to see ourselves in others: fragile people who want to feel loved and welcome.

Intimacy is an opportunity to develop our trust in God's living presence and a reminder of how close the risen Lord is to each of us.

**Ponder:** What fears inhibit me from being close to others?

**Prayer:** Risen Lord, your love unites the whole world. May your light teach me how to open my heart to the love of others.

**Practice:** Today I will invite someone to have a cup of tea with me.

# Saturday of the Octave of Easter

*Acts 4:13–21*
*Psalm 118:1 and 14–15ab, 16–18, 19–21*
*Mark 16:9–15*

**Now when they saw the boldness of Peter and John and realized that they were uneducated and ordinary men, they were amazed and recognized them as companions of Jesus.**

ACTS 4:13

*Reflection:* There is a trend in our world to impose uniformity on all people, to impose a kind of norm that precludes cultural differences, personal creativity, and individual quirkiness. Jesus, however, is forever countercultural and speaks and acts through the most unexpected of us.

We don't have to be ordained priests, biblical scholars, or trained theologians to be able to express the love of God in the world. We don't need a college degree, an executive position, or a famous name to be able to transform our world by our faith in Jesus.

Jesus calls ordinary people to extraordinary levels of service. Jesus sees into our hearts and knows we want to help those who are alone, ill, anxious, or despairing. Jesus places his mission of love and peace into our hands—ordinary, work-hardened, callused, and arthritic hands. We don't need manicures to be able to reach out and offer a loving hand to others. All we need is a desire to follow the will of God and the humility to ask God to show us what to do.

Our faith in Jesus gives us the power to make a difference in the world. Our faith in Jesus gives us the right words to speak at the right moment. Our faith in Jesus takes away our fear of deviating from a societal norm. Our faith in Jesus reminds us that we are called to make good use of our particular gifts and talents to help others. Our faith in Jesus helps us shine the light of hope and love in our corner of the universe.

*Ponder:* Whose faith amazes me?

*Prayer:* Risen Lord, you are our hope. Guide me in your ways that I may never be shy about speaking your words of love and peace.

*Practice:* Today I will volunteer to help with an adult-literacy program.

# Second Sunday of Easter

## YEAR A

---

*Acts 2:42–47*
*Psalm 118:2–4, 13–15, 22–24*
*1 Peter 1:3–9*
*John 20:19–31*

"Peace be with you. As the Father has sent me, so I send you." When [Jesus] had said this, he breathed on them and said to them, "Receive the Holy Spirit. If you forgive the sins of any, they are forgiven them; if you retain the sins of any, they are retained."

JOHN 20:21–23

**Reflection:** We need to be aware of the way we approach people. When we ignore people, they may feel disrespected or rejected. When we don't take time to listen to others, they may feel insignificant or unimportant. When we are angry and upset at people, they may feel abused or hurt. When we are impatient and frustrated with others, they may feel misunderstood or incompetent. When we are indifferent toward others, they may feel disheartened or discouraged.

After the resurrection, the first lesson Jesus teaches his disciples and us is how to approach people and life in general. He teaches us to approach our brothers and sisters with an attitude of peace. He shows us that God's peace does not violate or wound the dignity of others. God's peace has the power to remove the walls of fear, prejudice, and hatred of others. God's peace opens a pathway to mutual love and understanding.

In his person, the risen Jesus demonstrates embodied peace as a new way of living in the world. When we can approach humanity and creation with an embodied sense of peace and respect, we help to heal relationships among people and restore balance and harmony in the world. We have been given the Spirit of God and empowered to share forgiveness, the fruit of the resurrection. One of the greatest challenges of the Christian life is learning how to be a more authentic witness of the peace and forgiveness of God toward all people.

**Ponder:** How do I approach people throughout the day?

**Prayer:** Risen Lord, you share with me God's gifts of peace and forgiveness. Open my heart to share your peace and forgiveness with all people.

**Practice:** Today I will approach everyone in a kind and gentle manner.

# YEAR B

---

*Acts 4:32–35*
*Psalm 118:2–4, 13–15, 22–24*
*1 John 5:1–6*
*John 20:19–31*

**With great power the apostles gave their tes-
timony to the resurrection of the Lord Jesus,
and great grace was upon them all.**

ACTS 4:33

*Reflection:* We have been told on more than one
occasion that our actions speak louder than our
words. The way we act in life gives testimony to
what we believe and hold dear in our hearts.

It is hard to convince others to respond to the
needs of the poor if we are not involved in a project
that prepares a meal and feeds the poor. No one
will care to listen to us about visiting the sick and
lonely when we have not made the effort to visit a
hospital or nursing home. It is difficult to get others to advocate for peace and justice when we have
not resolved our personal conflicts with others. We
cannot preach to others about the love of God when
we harbor hatred and prejudice in our hearts.

After the resurrection, the followers of Christ
had to ensure that their preaching matched their

attitude and behavior. Preaching about the resurrection of the Lord Jesus required a new way of thinking and a new way of living. Belief in the resurrection challenged the followers of Christ to reflect on his life and ministry. They honored Jesus' teachings by following his example of reaching out to the poor, the rejected, the sick, and the lame. Their lives had to resemble the life of Christ, who came to bring God's compassion, love, peace, and forgiveness to all people.

Our actions, born out of faith in the resurrection of the Lord Jesus, have the power to change people's minds and hearts. People will know the love of God when we show love. People will know the mercy of God when we offer forgiveness. People will know the goodness of God when we are good to others.

*Ponder:* How often do my actions match my words?

*Prayer:* Risen Lord, you fulfilled your promise by rising from the dead. Help me to practice what I preach.

*Practice:* Today I will do more and speak less.

# YEAR C

---

*Acts 5:12–16*
*Psalm 118:2–4, 13–15, 22–24*
*Revelation 1:9–11a, 12–13, 17–19*
*John 20:19–31*

**Now many signs and wonders were done among the people through the apostles.**

ACTS 5:12

*Reflection:* Many signs and wonders are being performed by compassionate people in quiet and humble ways. We see people from all walks of life making a difference in the world every day. We see people in our community working together to build a home for a needy family. We see people working together to cook a meal to feed the hungry at a local soup kitchen. We see people working together to collect canned goods for a local food pantry. We see people working together to secure shelter for the homeless.

We see people from all over the world working together to rebuild communities devastated by earthquakes and hurricanes. We see people working together in poor countries to care for mothers and their children with AIDS. We see people working together to bring food and water to refugees affected by severe famine and drought. We see people of goodwill working together to protect the sacredness of life, to uphold the dignity of others, to promote human rights, to eradicate racism, violence, and human trafficking.

When Jesus rose from the dead, he gave his followers the power to work miracles—signs and wonders—among the people. Our belief in the resurrection is a statement of our willingness to allow the risen Lord to continue to work the signs and wonders of God through us. Empowered by our faith in the resurrection and inspired by the good works of so many good people around us, we are called to perform signs and wonders that help to rebuild people's lives, restore hope, and bring about peace.

*Ponder:* What signs and wonders have I done to help others?

*Prayer:* Risen Lord, your resurrection renewed the face of the earth and gave us hope. Make me eager to use my gifts and talents to rebuild people's lives and give them hope.

*Practice:* Today I will perform a small sign and wonder for someone in need.

# Monday of the Second Week of Easter

*Acts 4:23–31*
*Psalm 2:1–3, 4–7a, 7b–9*
*John 3:1–8*

**Jesus answered, "What is born of the flesh is flesh, and what is born of the Spirit is spirit."**

JOHN 3:6

***Reflection:*** Taking the time to align with God's will opens us to the power of the Spirit of God within us. God's will for us is to love our neighbor and to serve the needs of all. God's Spirit shows us how.

With a gentle word, we can stem an unjust tirade. With a firm "no," we can set a needed boundary. With a nod of encouragement, we can help someone succeed in life. With a welcoming smile, we can put someone at ease. With a serene outlook, we can find the patience to listen to someone we find difficult to understand. With compassionate arms, we can embrace those who are in pain and grief. With generous hands, we can bring food to the poor.

At every moment of the day or night, the Spirit is available to us. We don't have to stay stuck in a problem. We don't have to worry about finding the right words in a difficult situation. We don't have to force solutions and try to control outcomes. In our humanness, we think it is our job to figure things out. We forget the Spirit is God's gift to open our eyes to new possibilities and to show us how to grow in our likeness to God.

God's Spirit is ever present to hear our call for help, our need for strength, our plea for an understanding heart. God's Spirit shows us the way, gives us the courage, opens our mind and heart to compassion. When we ask the Spirit for guidance, we will be given the Spirit's own wisdom and know the next step to take.

**Ponder:** Where does the Spirit work in my life?

**Prayer:** Risen Lord, your Spirit enlightens the world. Teach me to ask for and trust the Spirit's guidance in every detail of my life.

**Practice:** Today I will ask the Spirit to show me what to do and how to do it.

# Tuesday of the
# Second Week of Easter

*Acts 4:32–37*
*Psalm 93:1ab, 1cd–2, 5*
*John 3:7b–15*

Jesus answered, "The wind blows where it chooses, and you hear the sound of it, but you do not know where it comes from or where it goes. So it is with everyone who is born of the Spirit."

JOHN 3:8

**Reflection:** We like being the center of attention and in control of situations because it makes us feel important and powerful. We like our personal freedom, independence, and self-autonomy. We like having options in life, making our own decisions, and experiencing life with minimum constraints. We like being able to self-manage and self-direct.

In our society, we are conditioned to believe that we are free and have control over our lives. We have a false sense of security because we have passwords and special codes to access our personal accounts, remote controls for our electronic devices, keys for the apartment, house, office, and car. Life is good until our passwords are compromised, our remote controls and keys are lost or stolen.

In the spiritual world, life is not about control but about trust in the Spirit of God, who empowers us to take risks, to surrender and be selfless. We are to be concerned about discerning and doing the will of God. In the spiritual world, we surrender to the mystery of God, trusting that the Spirit will show us the true way to love, happiness, and peace.

The resurrection of Jesus challenges us to trust the spiritual world more than the material world. In the spiritual world, we go where the breath of God leads us. Wherever we find ourselves, we must not be afraid to share the love, forgiveness, hope, and peace of the risen Lord.

The message of the resurrection is that life is good. Total peace and security come when we surrender to and trust the Spirit of God.

**Ponder:** Why am I afraid to surrender to and trust in the Spirit of God?

**Prayer:** Risen Lord, your Spirit guides us to peace and eternal life. Help me to trust that you are always with me on the journey of life.

**Practice:** Today I will trust my heart and not betray myself.

# Wednesday of the Second Week of Easter

*Acts 5:17–26*
*Psalm 34:2–3, 4–5, 6–7, 8–9*
*John 3:16–21*

**Jesus answered, "Indeed, God did not send the Son into the world to condemn the world, but in order that the world might be saved through him."**

JOHN 3:17

**Reflection:** Jesus is not here to condemn us. Jesus is here to love us. Jesus is here to make sure we understand the enormous, boundless love out of which God has made us. Jesus is here to teach us how to love ourselves, our enemies, and our neighbors with the same nonjudgmental, noncondemning love God has for us.

Upon awakening each day, we need to make choices: Shall we face the day with love or with fear? Shall we put our lives and wills into God's hands or try to control events and the people we encounter? Shall we look for the positive or dwell on the negative? Shall we be truthful and sincere or deceptive and superficial in our interactions with others? Shall we treat ourselves and others gently when we make mistakes or condemn our humanity?

Life is meant to be a continual adventure where we perfect our skills at loving God, ourselves, and others. Remembering that God loves the whole world, we can start by speaking courteously to all. We can listen respectfully to others' opinions and ideas. We can politely ask for help when we need it. We can thank others when they serve us a meal or wait on us in a store. We can send a message of hope to someone who is struggling with grief, depression, or loneliness.

Any time we make the effort to show love to any of God's children, we are honoring God with that same love. We have been sent by the risen Lord to manifest the deeply personal love God has for the world.

*Ponder:* How does God's love touch my life?

*Prayer:* Risen Lord, you prove the power of love over death. Help me to show love in my thoughts, words, and actions.

*Practice:* Today I will have a conversation with someone I usually avoid.

# Thursday of the Second Week of Easter

*Acts 5:27–33*
*Psalm 34:2 and 9, 17–18, 19–20*
*John 3:31–36*

**But Peter and the apostles answered, "We must obey God rather than any human authority."**

**ACTS 5:29**

*Reflection:* We follow certain laws to help keep order in our society: stop at a red light; don't serve alcohol to minors; don't plagiarize others' work; allow pedestrians the right of way; don't trespass on others' property. Many of our laws are variations on the laws God gave to Moses, the Ten Commandments. We are probably most familiar with "don't steal, don't lie, don't kill." The laws of God show us how to respect one another and ourselves.

Jesus taught us that the most important laws are to love God with all our heart, soul, and mind, and to love our neighbor as ourselves. As followers of Jesus, the law of love must always be our first choice.

When we confront difficulties in our daily lives, we must keep the law of love firmly in our minds. We must choose a response that is respectful, compassionate, and forgiving. When we have a decision to make, we must weigh the consequences of our decision in light of God's law of love. When friends invite us to do something that is risky, we must consider how God's law of love may guide us. When our families are struggling with conflicts, addictions, and the complexities of living in community, we must work together to find solutions that reflect God's law of love.

When we place our lives in God's loving care, take time to ask for God's guidance, and align our words and actions with God's law of love, we will find ourselves in intimate touch with our power to love and grow in God's likeness.

**Ponder:** When have I obeyed God's command to love?

**Prayer:** Risen Lord, your law is that we love one another. Help me to choose your law of love when I am perplexed.

**Practice:** Today I will take time to pray before making any decisions.

# Friday of the
# Second Week of Easter

*Acts 5:34–42*
*Psalm 27: 1, 4, 13–14*
*John 6:1–15*

**When Jesus realized that [the people] were about to come and take him by force to make him king, he withdrew again to the mountain by himself.**

JOHN 6:15

***Reflection:*** Being alone is preferable to being forced to do something that goes against God's will. Withdrawing from situations that threaten our ability to do the work of God is the sensible course of action. Seeking the wisdom of God is more challenging than following the dictates of the world.

We have no power over others' thoughts, words, or actions. We cannot control others' habits, emotions, or mental states. We cannot solve all the problems of the world. We cannot impose our will on others. We are not responsible for others' expectations of us.

We are responsible, however, for assessing situations and choosing the loving action. The loving action might be to allow others the freedom to make their own choices, even when we think they're making a mistake. The loving action might be to let others find their own solutions to their problems, even when we have advice to offer. The loving action might be to let others be who they are, even though we wish they were different. The loving action might be to take the time to confront someone with the truth of their harmful behavior.

A loving action that always works is to go to a quiet place where we can take the time to pray, be grounded in God's love, and ask God to show us what to do next. We know God will give us the courage and compassion to keep on loving, hoping, and serving others, even in the most difficult circumstances.

**Ponder:** When have I needed to withdraw and be alone?

**Prayer:** Risen Lord, you are our hope, our light, and our salvation. Teach me to gaze on your loveliness that I may be strengthened to keep on loving.

**Practice:** Today I will take a solitary walk and take refuge in the natural loveliness God has created.

# Saturday of the Second Week of Easter

*Acts 6:1–7*
*Psalm 33:1–2, 4–5, 18–19*
*John 6:16–21*

**The twelve said, "Therefore, friends, select from among yourselves seven men of good standing, full of the Spirit and of wisdom, whom we may appoint to this task, while we, for our part, will devote ourselves to prayer and to serving the word."**

**ACTS 6:3–4**

*Reflection:* In the early days of the Church, the whole community had the power to make decisions. The whole community had a say in who would have a leadership role. The whole community was trusted to choose helpers who were wise and full of the Spirit.

In any community of Christians, we must remember that we have been called to model leadership on the example of Jesus. Leadership means service, not privilege; humility, not arrogance. Leadership means collaboration, not domination; empowerment, not manipulation. Leadership means listening, not demanding.

A truly Christian community gives everyone a voice. A truly Christian community encourages participation. A truly Christian community reaches out to everyone in welcome. A truly Christian community serves the needs of the poor. A truly Christian community studies Scripture together. A truly Christian community helps its people develop relationships with God. A truly Christian community acknowledges the right of each member to question, explore, and discern God's will. A truly Christian community has God as its center, always open to the movement of the Spirit.

We have been called to follow the example of Jesus—to love, forgive, and bring the hope of God's merciful love to the world. We each have the responsibility to ensure that our Christian communities remain faithful to the example of Jesus. We need to remember that each of us is filled with the power of God's Spirit and that we are called to use that power for the good of all.

**Ponder:** When have I helped make decisions for my Christian community?

**Prayer:** Risen Lord, I place my trust in you. Fill me with your Spirit of hope and love. Teach me your wisdom.

**Practice:** Today I will not be afraid to respectfully voice my opinion.

# Third Sunday of Easter

## YEAR A

---

*Acts 2:14, 22–33*
*Psalm 16:1–2, 5, 7–8, 9–10, 11*
*1 Peter 1:17–21*
*Luke 24:13–35*

**While they were talking and discussing, Jesus himself came near and went with them, but their eyes were kept from recognizing him.**

LUKE 24:15–16

*Reflection:* A stranger is someone we do not know, a person outside our social group, neighborhood, or community. We do not do well when a stranger comes near us and wants to become a part of our lives. The stranger makes us feel vulnerable. In our mind, the stranger is the uninvited guest who disrupts our sense of comfort and security. Our instinct is to protect ourselves, prejudge, or avoid the person. We have no immediate desire to welcome and befriend the stranger.

As we mature, we learn that everyone is a stranger until we get to know the person on a deeper level. We seek courage to tame our fears because we see the value of companionship, mutual respect, and understanding. We realize that our ignorance keeps us from recognizing another's goodness and dignity.

After the resurrection Jesus came near his disciples, but they did not recognize him. In their eyes, Jesus was the uninvited stranger who walked into their grief and fear after the death of their friend. Jesus, the stranger, made them feel more vulnerable and uncomfortable. Yet as they walked together and listened to Jesus, the disciples' hearts were transformed. Jesus was no longer the uninvited stranger among them but the risen Lord. Jesus was now their intimate friend who gave them renewed hope, love, and peace.

The resurrection challenges us to get to know the risen Lord present in the Scriptures, in the Eucharist, and in humanity, especially the poor, the sick, and the lonely. The risen Lord teaches us to welcome the strangers among us and to show them the love and compassion of God.

**Ponder:** How do I treat strangers?

**Prayer:** Risen Lord, you walk with me as my friend and companion. Help me to recognize your presence in all people.

**Practice:** Today I will trust the Spirit and have a conversation with someone I do not know.

# YEAR B

---

*Acts 3:13–15, 17–19*
*Psalm 4:2, 4, 7–8, 9*
*1 John 2:1–5a*
*Luke 24:35–48*

**Whoever says, "I have come to know him," but does not obey his commandments, is a liar, and in such a person the truth does not exist; but whoever obeys his word, truly in this person the love of God has reached perfection.**

1 JOHN 2:4–5

*Reflection:* At times all of us are guilty of lying, deception, half-truths, gossip, and rumors. We lie because we are afraid—afraid that if others knew the truth about us, we would be rejected. We lie because we do not trust the truth. Each time we lie, we betray others as well as ourselves. With each lie, our character is tarnished, our spirit is divided, and our integrity is diminished. When we lie, we cannot be trusted.

Truth is at the heart of the human condition. We trust our elected officials to honor their oath of office. We trust our civic and business leaders to be honest stewards of the community's resources.

We trust our spiritual and religious leaders to practice what they preach. We trust our teachers and coaches to model fair play and good judgment.

The truth about God and humanity was revealed in the life of Jesus. Jesus was faithful to God, and God remained faithful to Jesus. The belief in the risen Jesus is a commitment to the truth about God: Life conquers death. Love overpowers hatred. Hope dispels darkness. Faith in the things of heaven brings us ultimate happiness and peace.

As followers of the risen Lord, we remain trustworthy when we respect the dignity of all people, defend the sacredness of life, and respond to the needs of the poor. Belief in the resurrection calls us to be truthful witnesses of love, peace, and compassion in the world.

**Ponder:** When do I find it hard to tell and live the truth?

**Prayer:** Risen Lord, your resurrection revealed to the world the hope and promise of new life. Help me to be a faithful, hopeful, loving presence to all people.

**Practice:** Today I will speak the truth in love.

# YEAR C

---

*Acts 5:27–32, 40b–41*
*Psalm 30:2, 4, 5–6, 11–12, 13*
*Revelation 5:11–14*
*John 21:1–19 or 21:1–14*

**Jesus came and took the bread and gave it to them, and did the same with the fish.**

JOHN 21:13

*Reflection:* Sometimes our pride, fear, and selfishness paralyze us. We feel uncomfortable around people who are suffering. We are too proud to be seen working in a soup kitchen with the poor and homeless. We are too afraid to associate with someone who is mentally ill or emotionally disturbed. We are too selfish to share some of our resources with the less fortunate.

Sometimes we are too self-righteous to forgive someone and too stubborn to change. We overpower people with our anger, bitterness, resentment, and jealousy. We don't want to give an inch and appear weak or powerless. We like being in control. We enjoy being the center of attention and getting our way.

In light of the resurrection, our life is supposed to be different. We are a new people in Christ.

We are called to be selfless, compassionate, kind, and generous. We are empowered to welcome all people, to serve the poor and needy with joy, to offer forgiveness from our heart, to care for the sick, and to work for peace.

After his resurrection, Jesus takes the initiative; he reaches out to his disciples. Although they betrayed him, he cares about them and is concerned about their mental, emotional, spiritual, and physical well-being. He wants to offer them forgiveness and peace; he wants them to heal. Preparing breakfast, he feeds them bread and fish. In feeding them, they remember him, and they remember his love and compassion.

Belief in the risen Jesus calls us to be like Jesus, to take the initiative and feed the hungry world with the bread of peace, love, compassion, and forgiveness.

**Ponder:** Where in my life do I lack initiative?

**Prayer:** Risen Lord, you gave your life to save the world. Help me to be a selfless servant of love and peace in the world.

**Practice:** Today I will visit a neighbor.

# Monday of the Third Week of Easter

*Acts 6:8–15*
*Psalm 119:23–24, 26–27, 29–30*
*John 6:22–29*

**Stephen, full of grace and power, did great wonders and signs among the people.**

**ACTS 6:8**

*Reflection:* The grace and power of God's Spirit direct Stephen in his work among the people. We, too, have been blessed with the grace and power of the Spirit through our baptism. We cannot deny this grace and power. We cannot claim in false modesty that we are not worthy. We cannot look to others for this grace and power. We must look deeply inside ourselves to discover how we may call upon the grace and power of the Spirit to do God's will and carry the message of God's hope, peace, compassion, and love to all people.

It is quite humbling to accept that God trusts us to find ways to make good use of the healing power of the Spirit in the world. It may take us some time to discern the best way to use this gift. Yet every day we can pour out the Spirit by intentionally choosing to follow Jesus' example of service, forgiveness, and unconditional love. Every day we can intentionally build our lives on a foundation of respect for others and ourselves. Every day we can intentionally look for ways to encourage others, to help those in need, and to share a word of hope wherever we go.

We may never know the "great wonders and signs" we bring to the world. We may never understand the impact of a kind word, a welcoming smile, a sincere expression of thanks. We may never see the results of a timely phone call, a note of condolence, or a demonstration of solidarity. We can trust, however, that when we allow the Spirit to guide us, our faith manifests God's own grace and love to all those we encounter.

**Ponder:** When have I let God's grace and power in me touch the lives of others?

**Prayer:** Risen Lord, your grace and love are all I need. Help me to do your will today.

**Practice:** Today I will thank God for the gift of the Holy Spirit in me.

# Tuesday of the Third Week of Easter

*Acts 7:51—8:1a*
*Psalm 31:3cd–4, 6 and 7b and 8a, 17 and 21ab*
*John 6:30–35*

**Then Jesus said to them, "Very truly, I tell you, it was not Moses who gave you the bread from heaven, but it is my Father who gives you the true bread from heaven."**

JOHN 6:32

*Reflection:* Jesus is our spiritual nourishment. When we are hungry for comfort, companionship, or encouragement, we can go to Jesus to be fed. When we are hungry for justice, honesty, or reconciliation, we can go to Jesus to be fed. When we are hungry for understanding, compassion, or love, we can go to Jesus to be fed.

When we are thirsty for truth, freedom, and equality, Jesus guides us. When we are thirsty for kindness, respect, and acceptance, Jesus supplies us. When we are thirsty for unity, harmony, and peace, Jesus leads us.

As Jesus nourishes us, so we must nourish others. We must intentionally choose to be those who offer comfort, kindness, and encouragement. We must be those who demand justice and equality. We must be those who work for unity, peace, and understanding.

We are the nourishing hands of God in our world. People will come to know Jesus by observing our words and actions. People will come to understand the infinite patience, mercy, and forgiveness of Jesus by interacting with us. People will come to hope in Jesus' love and personal care for each of us by experiencing it at our hands.

It is our calling to tell the story of hope that Jesus embodies. It is our task to practice the words, actions, and behaviors that tell that story. It is our joy and privilege to become more like Jesus as we grow in love and forgiveness.

Jesus is the bread of life—and we are those who make sure that bread of hope and love is distributed equally to all of God's people.

*Ponder:* How does Jesus feed me?

*Prayer:* Risen Lord, you shine your kindness on all people everywhere. Help me to feed those who need your love.

*Practice:* Today I will feed the people I meet with a serving of kindness and respect.

# Wednesday of the Third Week of Easter

*Acts 8:1b–8*
*Psalm 66:1–3a, 4–5, 6–7a*
*John 6:35–40*

**Jesus said to them, "I am the bread of life. Whoever comes to me will never be hungry, and whoever believes in me will never be thirsty."**

JOHN 6:35

*Reflection:* We live in a culture that thrives on our hunger and thirst for instant gratification. We spend a lot of time driving from place to place looking for something to eat, drink, or wear. Our money is used to support our physical cravings. No matter what we buy, it never seems to be enough. We always want more. We possess an abundance of material things, but we still feel empty and unsatisfied inside.

Life becomes very superficial when we begin to define ourselves by the food we eat, the beverages we drink, the clothes we wear, and the car we drive. The meaning and purpose of life cannot be purchased at a store. Our ultimate happiness and peace cannot be found in material things. The essence of life is spiritual. Our hearts long for inner spiritual peace. The Christian heart longs for communion with God.

Jesus tells us that he is "the bread of life" who satisfies our spiritual hunger and thirst. The Word of God is the food and drink of the Christian spiritual life. When we eat and drink of the Word of God, we experience an inner peace and satisfaction that the world cannot give. We come to discover that God's Word gives our lives meaning and purpose.

Our belief in the resurrection redirects our lives to love God and neighbor. As we feed on the Word of God, we become transformed into the image of the risen Jesus. With a selfless, generous spirit, we take the initiative to feed those who hunger and thirst.

**Ponder:** What is my spiritual hunger and thirst?

**Prayer:** Risen Lord, you are the bread of life that satisfies my life. Help me to be more attentive to the health of my spiritual life.

**Practice:** Today I will take an inventory of my spiritual needs.

# Thursday of the Third Week of Easter

*Acts 8:26–40*
*Psalm 66:8–9, 16–17, 20*
*John 6:44–51*

**Jesus answered them, "It is written in the prophets, 'And they shall all be taught by God.'"**

JOHN 6:45

*Reflection:* God is our primary teacher. From Jesus, we learn to be like God. We learn to forgive those who have hurt us. We learn to show compassion to those who are suffering. We learn to let go of grudges and be reconciled with those we resent. We learn to accept others as they are. We learn to love others without expecting anything in return.

Jesus teaches us how to be in this world. We learn to put God at the center of our daily lives. We learn to ask to be shown God's will for us and to trust that God will show us what to do and how to do it. We learn to take time alone for prayer and meditation to renew ourselves in God's infinite love and comfort. We learn to spend time reading and reflecting on Scripture to deepen our relationship with the Word.

Jesus teaches us how to relate to others. We learn to care for the poor, the lonely, the marginalized, the abandoned, and those whom society has labeled a misfit. We learn to share our time, our material goods, and our talents with those in need. We learn to stand against war, hatred, hypocrisy, and greed.

We all have the same teacher: a loving God. All of us have the opportunity to become like God in joy, love, and goodness. All of us have the opportunity to deepen and widen our relationship with God. All of us have the opportunity to relate to others with the loving, respectful attitude of God.

**Ponder:** What has God taught me about myself?

**Prayer:** Risen Lord, you have blessed me with the gift of life. Help me to use this precious gift to share your hope, joy, compassion, and love in the world.

**Practice:** Today I will spend five minutes alone with God as my teacher.

# Friday of the
# Third Week of Easter

*Acts 9:1–20*
*Psalm 117:1bc, 2*
*John 6:52–59*

**Meanwhile Saul, still breathing threats and murder against the disciples of the Lord, went to the high priest and asked him for letters to the synagogues at Damascus, so that if he found any who belonged to the Way, men or women, he might bring them bound to Jerusalem.**

ACTS 9:1–2

**Reflection:** Sometimes we are so convinced we are right. We are positive our outlook is the right one. We are sure our opinion is correct. We are confident we know better than others. We are assured, definite, and self-righteous.

But are we happy? Are we joy-filled? Kind? Respectful? Courteous? Understanding? Forgiving? Have we stopped and really listened to others? Have we opened our minds and hearts to new ideas? Have we stopped being teachable?

When we deliberately take the time to consider what others are doing or saying, we often realize that deep down we have a fear of attitudes, lifestyles, traditions, or opinions that are different from ours. We fear that our safety and all that is familiar may be taken away from us. Instead of being receptive to new ideas, we shut them off, ignore them, or like Saul, persecute those who support them.

Having opinions or beliefs is not necessarily harmful. But when we become so attached to our sense of what is right that we treat others with disrespect, contempt, or violence, it's time to rethink our position.

As followers of Jesus, we need always be humble and grounded in love. When we voice our opinion or urge a certain action, we need to ask ourselves, Do these words reflect respect for others? Does this action reflect God's love for all people? How important is it to be right?

**Ponder:** Would I rather be right or be loving?

**Prayer:** Risen Lord, faith, hope, and love are your good news. Bless me with an open mind and receptive heart that I may share your good news with all the world.

**Practice:** Today I will listen respectfully when others share their opinions.

# Saturday of the Third Week of Easter

*Acts 9:31–42*
*Psalm 116:12–13, 14–15, 16–17*
*John 6:60–69*

**So Jesus asked the twelve, "Do you also wish to go away?" Simon Peter answered him, "Lord, to whom can we go? You have the words of eternal life. We have come to believe and know that you are the Holy One of God."**

JOHN 6:67–69

***Reflection:*** Having spent months and months with Jesus, the Twelve have learned to believe in his words because they have seen him in action, and his actions bear witness to what he preaches. Their minds and hearts have gradually awakened to know him as the Christ. They have now made the decision to put their whole selves—their thoughts and feelings, their very lives—into his care.

The decision to trust God is not always easy to reach. Sometimes the people in our lives have hurt us physically, mentally, emotionally, and spiritually. Sometimes our suffering has been so deep that we have retreated behind a protective wall where we think we are safe from harm. We make the unconscious resolve to never trust anyone again.

Yet the Spirit within us is constantly encouraging us to come out from behind the wall. The Spirit leads us to people who will love and accept us as we are, giving us new chances to learn to trust again. As we learn to trust other people, our trust in God deepens. We become aware of God's movement in our lives, aware of God in the world around us, aware of God in others. We gradually take down our protective wall and open fully to life and the love and joy it has to offer. We learn to turn to God with all our longings, and we come to know that God will give us everything we need.

**Ponder:** Can God trust me?

**Prayer:** Risen Lord, you give me everything I need and long for. Teach me to call on you when I am suffering. Help me to believe and know you answer me.

**Practice:** Today I will ask God for what I want and need, and then let go of the outcome.

# Fourth Sunday of Easter

## YEAR A

---

*Acts 2:14a, 36–41*
*Psalm 23:1–3a, 3b–4, 5, 6*
*1 Peter 2:20b–25*
*John 10:1–10*

Jesus said to them, "The one who enters by the gate is the shepherd of the sheep. The gatekeeper opens the gate for him, and the sheep hear his voice. He calls his own sheep by name and leads them out. When he has brought out all his own, he goes ahead of them, and the sheep follow him because they know his voice."

JOHN 10:2–4

***Reflection:*** It takes time to develop our own voice. Our voice conveys what is hidden in our heart. With our voice we can be in solidarity with others. With our voice we can encourage people to do good for others. We can call them to care for the sick, feed the poor, visit prisoners, clothe the naked, and shelter the homeless.

With our voice we can help people to be healthy. We can alert them to harmful behaviors, encourage them to eat less, exercise, and get plenty of sleep. With our voice we can advocate for the voiceless. We can speak out against exploitation of the poor, child abuse, racial discrimination, war, and violence. With our voice we can bring about change.

The risen Jesus is the Good Shepherd who speaks with the voice of God. Those who listen to the Good Shepherd follow the way of love, compassion, peace, understanding, and forgiveness. We know that the Shepherd behind the voice protects us and keeps us safe from all harm.

Belief in the risen Jesus says that the quiet voice of the Good Shepherd overpowers the voices of the world; that the voice of life, love, compassion, and peace drowns out the voices of death, hatred, selfishness, and violence. We are called to shepherd one another with the voice of God and lead all people to the gate of eternal life.

**Ponder:** How do I shepherd others?

**Prayer:** Risen Lord, you are the Good Shepherd who leads me along safe paths. Help me to be a good shepherd to all people.

**Practice:** Today I will use my voice on behalf of the defenseless.

# YEAR B

---

*Acts 4:8–12*
*Psalm 118:1, 8–9, 21–23, 26, 28, 29*
*1 John 3:1–2*
*John 10:11–18*

**"I am the good shepherd. The good shepherd lays down his life for the sheep."**

JOHN 10:11

**Reflection:** We need good role models to teach us how to become mature, caring, and responsible persons. Good parents model mutual love, understanding, self-control, respect for others, kind speech, and concern for the needy. Good teachers model a passion for teaching, fairness in the classroom, civility, a love of knowledge, and the search for truth. Good nurses model care, teamwork, and prudence. Good public officials model strong leadership, ethical behavior, and concern for the common good. Good spiritual leaders model humble service, trustworthiness, and compassion for all people.

When we refuse to be models of goodness, love, compassion, and peace for one another, we know what happens in our families, in our communities, in the marketplaces, and in the world. Life is threatened, peace and security are compromised, the weak are overpowered, the needs of the poor are ignored, relationships are broken, and people are unwilling to work together for the good of all.

Jesus tells us that he is the Good Shepherd who watches over us, protecting us from harm. Jesus assures us of his unconditional love. He will never abandon us and offers his life as a gift so that we may live.

Jesus invites us to live in the uncomfortable manner of the Good Shepherd. We are called to risk our lives for the sake of others. Our belief in the resurrection means we are willing to risk being the good shepherds of love, compassion, forgiveness, and peace when the forces of hatred, selfishness, resentment, and violence tear our world apart.

*Ponder:* How can I be a better role model in my community?

*Prayer:* Risen Lord, you are the Good Shepherd who watches over us and protects us from all harm. Give me the courage to be a loving shepherd and advocate for the poor and vulnerable.

*Practice:* Today I will model goodness, humility, and kind speech.

# YEAR C

———————

*Acts 13:14, 43–52*
*Psalm 100:1–2, 3, 5*
*Revelation 7:9, 14b–17*
*John 10:27–30*

**After this I looked, and there was a great multitude that no one could count, from every nation, from all tribes and peoples and languages, standing before the throne and before the Lamb, robed in white, with palm branches in their hands.**

<small>REVELATION 7:9</small>

*Reflection:* As we grow and mature, we realize we need a vision of life to hold our world together. A vision of life is the lens through which we see the world, define who we are, discern our purpose on this earth, shape our values, and relate to others. Our vision of life gives us a sense of direction and a framework to interpret our human experiences.

Our vision of life evolves from our interaction with nature and the diverse people around us. Our vision of life is expressed through our words and actions. We tweak our vision of life by praying and meditating on Scripture, reading poetry and literature, listening to music, studying art, and engaging in a variety of creative activities.

God's vision for the world is revealed in the resurrection. It is a vision of hope and new life. The resurrection of Jesus is the lens through which Christians ought to see and interpret the human condition. The resurrection redefines who we are and our purpose in life. Our belief in the resurrection obliges us to live out of God's vision for humanity: a vision of a great multitude from every nation, race, people, and tongue living together in unity, peace, and love.

When we allow God's vision to take root in our hearts and transform our lives, we participate in God's work of renewing creation and the face of the earth.

**Ponder:** What is my vision of life?

**Prayer:** Risen Lord, your resurrection gives me hope and the promise of new life. Open my heart to embrace and share your vision of love and peace with all people.

**Practice:** Today I will reflect on the meaning and significance of the resurrection in my life.

# Monday of the Fourth Week of Easter

*Acts 11:1–18*
*Psalm 42:2–3; 43:3, 4*
*John 10:1–10 or 10:11–18*

**Peter began to explain, "And as I began to speak, the Holy Spirit fell upon them just as it had upon us at the beginning."**

**ACTS 11:15**

*Reflection:* God's Spirit goes where it wants and arrives when it is least expected. The Spirit fills the hearts of all as God wishes. The Spirit touches the lives of all as God commands. The Spirit enlightens the minds of all as God desires.

God's Spirit is not exclusive. The Spirit has the power to touch all people everywhere.

God's Spirit is not prejudiced. The Spirit sees all people with the heart of love and compassion.

God's Spirit is not indifferent. The Spirit lightens the lives of the poor, the ill, the homeless, the lost, the alienated, and the rejected.

God's Spirit is not biased. The Spirit favors all people equally.

God's Spirit is not stingy. The Spirit pours out love, joy, comfort, creativity, and hope to all people with abundant generosity.

God's Spirit is not proud. The Spirit enters the lives of the humble, the arrogant, the fearful, the courageous, the wealthy, the impoverished, the privileged, the outcast.

God's Spirit is not under our control. The Spirit moves according to God's will.

By our baptism, we have been graced with the gift of the Holy Spirit. With the Spirit to guide us, we, too, can mold our lives according to God's will of love, compassion, and respect for all people. We can pour out our gifts generously to serve the needs of others. We can shed the light of comfort, harmony, and dignity by our words and actions. We can bring hope to those who are despairing. We can treat all people with equal favor.

**Ponder:** When has God's Holy Spirit surprised me?

**Prayer:** Risen Lord, your Spirit moves within the hearts of all people. May I let your light, love, faith, and hope lead me all the days of my life.

**Practice:** Today I will let go of expectations and observe the surprises the Spirit has in store for me.

# Tuesday of the
# Fourth Week of Easter

*Acts 11:19–26*
*Psalm 87:1b–3, 4–5, 6–7*
*John 10:22–30*

**Jesus answered, "My sheep hear my voice. I know them, and they follow me."**

**JOHN 10:27**

*Reflection:* Jesus knows us. He knows our vulnerability. He knows our innocence. He knows our goodness.

Jesus knows our struggles to be kind and patient. He knows our efforts to be generous and forgiving. He knows our intention to be respectful and courteous.

Jesus knows our need for love and our longing to be whole. He knows we depend on him for guidance. He knows we are lost without his gentle touch and encouraging presence.

Jesus knows, loves, and accepts us just as we are. He lets us hear his voice so that we know where to follow him.

We hear the voice of Jesus in sacred Scripture. We listen to the Word to learn how to be more like Jesus. We reflect on the Word to discern what is being spoken to us in the moment. We study the Word to develop our relationship with Jesus and to come to know him more intimately.

We hear the voice of Jesus in our own hearts. We hear the silent call to holiness. We hear the hushed reminder to pray and give thanks to God. We hear the quiet invitation to love and be compassionate.

Sometimes we cannot hear Jesus' voice even though we take time to listen carefully. Instead of becoming discouraged or thinking we have been abandoned, we can work on trusting the silence of God. We can rely on all that we have learned about patience, kindness, compassion, forgiveness, and hope—and keep on with our lives. We can keep on reaching out to help those in need. We can keep on loving our enemies. We can keep on visiting the lonely. We can keep on trusting our hearts and showing our goodness and love to the world.

*Ponder:* When do I hear and follow Jesus?

*Prayer:* Risen Lord, your voice is gentle and reassuring. Open my ears to hear your word of love. Help me to trust and follow you.

*Practice:* Today I will listen for the voice of Jesus before making any decisions.

# Wednesday of the Fourth Week of Easter

*Acts 12:24—13:5a*
*Psalm 67:2–3, 5, 6 and 8*
*John 12:44–50*

**Then Jesus cried aloud, "...for I have not spoken on my own, but the Father who sent me has himself given me a commandment about what to say and what to speak. And I know that his commandment is eternal life. What I speak, therefore, I speak just as the Father has told me."**

JOHN 12:44, 49–50

**Reflection:** All that Jesus teaches points us to eternal life. We hear Jesus speak about how blessed are the peacemakers, the merciful, and the pure of heart. We hear Jesus speak about forgiving those who have hurt us and loving our enemies. We hear Jesus speak about how we need to let our light of goodness shine in the world.

All of Jesus' interchanges with people point us to eternal life. We hear Jesus speak words of welcome to Zaccheus. We hear Jesus speak words of rebuke to hypocritical spiritual leaders. We hear

Jesus speak words of hope and encouragement to the repentant thief.

All of Jesus' prayers point us to God, who gives us eternal life. We hear Jesus speak the word "Abba" and we know God as our Father. We hear Jesus pray to do God's will even in the face of crucifixion. We hear Jesus call to God in his pain and distress on the cross.

All of Jesus' actions speak of eternal life. Jesus speaks of healing and compassion by touching those with leprosy, those who are blind, deaf, and lame. Jesus speaks of acceptance and inclusion by sharing meals with people from all walks of life. Jesus speaks of hope and new life by bringing Jairus' daughter and Lazarus back from death—and by rising from the dead himself.

Jesus speaks with words and actions to show us the many different ways to follow the pathway of love, the pathway to eternal life.

**Ponder:** How does Jesus speak eternal life to me?

**Prayer:** Risen Lord, you speak of words of hope to the world. Help me to hear your words of eternal life and put them into practice.

**Practice:** Today I will speak loving words to my family, friends, and coworkers.

# Thursday of the Fourth Week of Easter

*Acts 13:13–25*
*Psalm 89:2–3, 21–22, 25 and 27*
*John 13:16–20*

**Jesus said to them, "Very truly, I tell you, servants are not greater than their master, nor are messengers greater than the one who sent them."**

JOHN 13:16

***Reflection:*** We remember the people who made a positive impact on our lives. We reflect on the lessons they taught us and teach them to others. Because they are an integral part of our lives, we catch ourselves repeating their favorite expressions and imitating certain behaviors. These great teachers of life gave of themselves so that we could have a good self-image and develop our own gifts and talents. They showed us how to be humble of heart and generous in serving the needs of others.

Whatever gifts and talents we possess, they are to be used generously in service of others. When we share what we have with a humble heart, we will gain a greater understanding of the human condition, respect and compassion for others, and a sense of peace. These are the hopeful signs that appear when we are driven by a spirit of service rather than a spirit of competition.

Our belief in the resurrection prompts us to reflect on the life of the risen Jesus. Jesus teaches his disciples to be humble, to serve others, and to be messengers of hope, love, forgiveness, and peace to all nations. The risen Jesus is our great teacher of selfless love and humble service. We are called to imitate Jesus' example of humble service and to share his teachings with believers and unbelievers alike. The great challenge of the Christian spiritual life is not to be greater than our Teacher, but to be *like* our Teacher. When we think and act like the risen Jesus, the world is transformed and renewed in hope.

**Ponder:** How can I be a humble, generous servant in my community?

**Prayer:** Risen Lord, you came to serve and not to be served. Help me to be more humble of heart and less competitive toward others.

**Practice:** Today I will try to be quiet and inconspicuous.

# Friday of the Fourth Week of Easter

*Acts 13:26–33*
*Psalm 2:6–7, 8–9, 10–11ab*
*John 14:1–6*

**Jesus answered, "Do not let your hearts be troubled. Believe in God, believe also in me."**

JOHN 14:1

*Reflection:* Many happenings in our world trouble our hearts. We have constant access to instantaneous news bites about riots, wars, child abuse, natural disasters, and meteoric disturbances. The media serves up stories that horrify, terrify, and deplete our hope in humankind. On a more intimate scale, our family situation can trouble our hearts as well. Some family members persist in risky behavior. Some family members treat us with disrespect. Some family members are gravely ill. Some family members have turned away from the compassion and comfort of God.

Jesus tells us we have the choice and the power to keep our hearts from being troubled. We do not have to let the problems of the world, the problems of our family and friends, or our own problems disturb our serenity. When we fix our thoughts on

God and put our lives and will into God's compassionate care, we let go of our need to control life events. We learn to trust that God is in charge and will not let us down. We come to believe that God has a vision for the world that is good, pure, and loving.

We come to know we have a part to play in that vision by living in the hope of Easter. The hope of Easter is the triumph of life over death. The hope of Easter is the triumph of light over darkness. The hope of Easter is the triumph of love over fear.

With the hope of Easter to sustain us, we find the courage to keep our hearts focused on believing in God's unconditional love for all of humankind.

**Ponder:** What troubles my heart at the moment?

**Prayer:** Risen Lord, you are the way that leads us to eternal life. Help me to believe in you. Heal my unbelief.

**Practice:** Today I will write a note to God about something that has been troubling me. I will ask for the faith to let God handle it.

# Saturday of the Fourth Week of Easter

*Acts 13:44–52*
*Psalm 98:1, 2–3ab, 3cd–4*
*John 14:7–14*

**Jesus answered, "I will do whatever you ask in my name, so that the Father may be glorified in the Son. If in my name you ask me for anything, I will do it."**

JOHN 14:13–14

*Reflection:* We have all had the experience of prayers that seem to go unanswered or prayers that are answered differently than what we had hoped or expected. Yet we ask in the name of Jesus—why doesn't he do what we ask?

Jesus is God's Word made flesh. Jesus is Love incarnate. Whatever we ask in the name of Jesus must be asked in love. Whatever we ask in the name of Jesus must be from our hearts, from the vulnerability of our dependence on God, from the knee-bending knowledge of our human limitations.

Anything we ask in the name of Jesus must come from a humble heart. We must be open to God's will. We must be ready to be shown what to do and how to do it. We must be ready to let go of our need to control people, places, things, and the events of life.

Anything we ask in the name of Jesus must come from a belief that it will be done according to God's will. We must have faith in God's timing. We must have the hope that God is listening. We must have the trust that God knows the best way to fulfill our needs.

Anything we ask in the name of Jesus must come from our love of God, the love of ourselves, and the love of our neighbors. When we ask for anything in the name of love, from the place of love, we know Jesus will do it.

**Ponder:** What do I ask in the name of Jesus?

**Prayer:** Risen Lord, you reveal your love and compassion to us in every moment. Help me to pray from my heart, with hope and trust in your loving response.

**Practice:** Today I will search my heart and ask in the name of Jesus for something I really need or want, however small or silly it seems.

# Fifth Sunday of Easter

## YEAR A

———

*Acts 6:1–7*
*Psalm 33:1–2, 4–5, 18–19*
*1 Peter 2:4–9*
*John 14:1–12*

**Jesus said, "Do not let your hearts be troubled. Believe in God, believe also in me. In my Father's house there are many dwelling-places."**

JOHN 14:1–2

***Reflection:*** We do not have the luxury of living undisturbed, untroubled lives. Our hearts are full of sadness when we are confronted with pain, suffering, and tragedy. Our hearts are full of sadness when we are faced with the death of a family member or close friend. Our hearts are full of sadness when bullying and violence overtake our schools and neighborhoods. Our hearts are full of sadness at the sight of starving children, people ravaged by HIV/AIDS, refugees on the run from genocide and war, people left homeless after earthquakes, hurricanes, and storms. Our hearts are full of sadness when there is disregard for life and disrespect toward people from different races and cultures.

Without faith in God, it is difficult to deal with the difficulties and struggles of life. We give up on living and succumb to despair, defeat, and death. Without faith in the resurrection of Jesus, we have no hope, no future, and no way out of our chaotic, troubled lives.

When our hearts are full of sadness, we long for someone to offer us love, compassion, understanding, encouragement, and peace. We want to dwell in a place of total safety and security. In the resurrection, God satisfies our longing with the gift of his risen Son. We are invited to dwell in happiness and love with the risen Jesus. With faith in the risen Jesus, our troubled hearts are transformed into hearts of love and peace. We can walk with blessed assurance and hope that we have a dwelling place with God in heaven.

*Ponder:* What is the source of my sadness?

*Prayer:* Risen Jesus, you heal our broken hearts and give us peace. Help me to be a source of encouragement to those troubled by pain and suffering.

*Practice:* Today I will not allow the problems of life to overwhelm my heart.

# YEAR B

---

*Acts 9:26–31*
*Psalm 22:26–27, 28, 30, 31–32*
*1 John 3:18–24*
*John 15:1–8*

Jesus answered him, "Abide in me as I abide in you. Just as the branch cannot bear fruit by itself unless it abides in the vine, neither can you unless you abide in me. I am the vine, you are the branches. Those who abide in me and I in them bear much fruit, because apart from me you can do nothing."

JOHN 15:4–5

**Reflection:** The family is the place where we discover who we are, form our attitudes about life, and learn how to live with others. Our experiences in the family stay with us; they are part of the fabric of our lives. Whatever we say and do in life reflects our family values. We know that it is difficult to progress in life apart from a caring and loving family. We rely on our family to give us a firm foundation to succeed in life.

Beyond the family, we need a community to give us a deeper sense of belonging. We need the emotional and spiritual support of friends to walk with us through the various twists and turns of life. Our experiences with our friends and neighbors stay with us; they are part of the fabric of our lives. Within the life of a community, we learn how to become committed, compassionate, loving, forgiving, and faithful persons. We rely heavily on a loving and supportive community to sustain us in times of trial.

We also need to be in communion with the risen Jesus to live a holy life. We meet the risen Jesus in the gospels, in the Eucharist, in prayer, and in the poor. These experiences stay with us; they are part of the fabric of our lives. Our new life in the risen Jesus is reflected in the way we treat others. With the risen Jesus we can bear God's fruit of love, compassion, peace, and forgiveness in the world.

*Ponder:* How do I abide in the risen Jesus?

*Prayer:* Risen Jesus, your abiding presence gives us hope. Help me to be a loving presence to others.

*Practice:* Today I will abide with God in prayer for ten minutes.

# YEAR C

---

*Acts 14:21–27*
*Psalm 145:8–9, 10–11, 12–13*
*Revelation 21:1–5a*
*John 13:31–33a, 34–35*

Jesus said, "I give you a new commandment,
that you love one another. Just as I have loved
you, you also should love one another. By this
everyone will know that you are my disciples,
if you have love for one another."

JOHN 13:34–35

*Reflection:* We keep repeating the same old negative behaviors. We do not treat others fairly. We become angry and resentful. We compete and fight
with others. We take sides and cause division. We
bully people to get our own way. We gossip and
distort the truth. We say and do hurtful things. We
discriminate against people because of their race,
gender, religion, culture, nationality, social back-
ground, or sexual orientation. We are self-centered
and arrogant. We are indifferent to the needs of the
poor.

Our old attitudes and patterns of behavior
dominate our lives. We think it is impossible to
change. We lack the willpower to liberate ourselves

from the negative thinking that results in the mistreatment of others. We fail to see that the way we treat people reveals our outlook on life and the wounded nature of our hearts. We continue to convey a message of distrust and fear of others.

Jesus gives us a new commandment, a new outlook on life, another way to relate to people. Jesus tells us that God's love changes us inwardly and makes everything new. We begin to see the world and people through the lens of God's transforming love. When we surrender ourselves to God's love, we become God's gift of love to others. The resurrection of Jesus conveys a message of love and hope for humanity. It challenges us to allow our hearts to be dominated by the power of God's love. We become the real presence of the risen Jesus in the world when we love one another.

**Ponder:** What attitudes and behaviors do I need to change in my life?

**Prayer:** Risen Jesus, you command us to love as you have loved. Cleanse my heart of pride, selfishness, and prejudice so that I may love unconditionally.

**Practice:** Today I will approach people with an attitude of love and respect.

# Monday of the Fifth Week of Easter

*Acts 14:5–18*
*Psalm 115:1–2, 3–4, 15–16*
*John 14:21–26*

**Jesus answered, "But the Advocate, the Holy Spirit, whom the Father will send in my name, will teach you everything, and remind you of all that I have said to you."**

**JOHN 14:26**

***Reflection:*** The Holy Spirit moves with us as we go about our daily activities. The Spirit breathes with us moment to moment. Our challenge is to stay aware of how the Holy Spirit is moving from moment to moment and to go with the Spirit's flow.

The Holy Spirit has much to teach us about making choices that reflect our likeness to God's love and goodness. The Holy Spirit is the whispered reminder to be patient with those who aggravate us. The Holy Spirit is the gentle nudge to respond generously to the needs of the poor. The Holy Spirit is the impulse to reach out in compassion to those who are sad, ill, lonely, tired, and in need of a friendly presence.

When we say the Our Father as Jesus taught us, it is the Holy Spirit in us that reminds us to pray. When we intentionally seek to love our enemies as Jesus taught us, it is the Holy Spirit in us that reminds us to open our hearts to all of God's people. When we give shelter to the homeless and visit the sick and imprisoned, it is the Holy Spirit in us that reminds us that all people are made in the image and likeness of God and are worthy of respect.

The Holy Spirit is God's gift to us so that we can live in hope, knowing we are never alone, and confident that the power of God is as close to us as our next breath.

*Ponder:* What does the Holy Spirit teach me?

*Prayer:* Risen Lord, you have blessed us with abundant gifts. Open my ears to hear the teaching of the Holy Spirit that I may use these gifts to bring hope, peace, and love to those in need.

*Practice:* Today I will ask the Holy Spirit to teach me compassion for those living in war-stricken lands.

# Tuesday of the Fifth Week of Easter

*Acts 14:19–28*
*Psalm 145:10–11, 12–13ab, 21*
*John 14:27–31a*

**Jesus answered, "Peace I leave with you; my peace I give to you. I do not give to you as the world gives. Do not let your hearts be troubled, and do not let them be afraid."**

**Reflection:** Jesus gives with open hands and open arms. Jesus gives unconditionally. Jesus gives from a heart overflowing with peace, love, and compassion.

Our experience of giving may be different. We may give as the world gives. We may give in hopes for a return. We may be resentful when we give and no one says thank-you. We may be discouraged when we give and no one notices or cares.

We may have been on the receiving end of someone's giving. We may have been indifferent to or critical of what was given to us. We may have expected more and been disappointed at what was given to us. We may have forgotten to look beyond the gift and see the heart of the giver.

*Fifth Week of Easter* 83

Jesus gives us his peace freely. When we receive this gift in the manner in which it is offered, we recognize that we are privileged to share it with others. We share peace in our daily activities when we treat all people with respect, refuse to enter into conflict with others, and promote justice toward all people everywhere. We share peace when we speak out against war, defend the right to have a person's resources used for peaceful purposes, and support programs that counteract racism, poverty, and the influence of gangs.

The peace of Jesus is a powerful gift. His peace is the serenity that comes from giving without wanting or needing a return. His peace is the joy that comes from loving without conditions. His peace is the hope for a world where all people live free of greed, indifference, dissatisfaction, resentment, and fear.

**Ponder:** How do I receive the gift of the peace of Jesus?

**Prayer:** Risen Lord, you have given us your peace. Teach me to share your peace wisely and without conditions.

**Practice:** Today I will practice peace with every step I take.

# Wednesday of the Fifth Week of Easter

*Acts 15:1–6*
*Psalm 122:1–2, 3–4ab, 4cd–5*
*John 15:1–8*

**Jesus answered, "I am the vine, you are the branches. Those who abide in me and I in them bear much fruit, because apart from me you can do nothing."**

JOHN 15:5

**Reflection:** A vine rooted in rich soil produces many offshoots, many branches that will bear the fruit of the vine. The branches cannot exist without the vine to feed them.

Jesus uses an example from the people's agricultural experience to explain our dependence on God—and God's hope in us. We are inextricably entwined with God. With this interdependence come the grace, the power, and the calling to be a living reminder of God's presence in our world. We always have the choice to opt out of our calling, yet such a choice hinders us from bearing the rich fruits of hope, peace, compassion, and love in the world.

As a fruit-bearing branch on the Jesus vine, we draw nourishment from the Scriptures, taking the time to study the teachings, words, and actions of Jesus and imitating his example as best we can. We intentionally nourish ourselves by choosing forgiveness over resentment, peace over conflict, hope over despair, and love over fear.

Reflecting on the powerful prayer life of Jesus, we feed ourselves by spending intimate moments in conscious contact with God. We seek to know God's will for us so that we are constantly aware of God's loving presence as we work to fulfill God's vision of a world where love and peace unite all people.

Meditating on Jesus' triumph over death, we cultivate a hopeful outlook, a willingness to embrace the mystery of life, and a joyful presence for others. Our work unites us more intimately with God and bears rich and satisfying fruit in the world.

**Ponder:** What fruit do I bear in the world?

**Prayer:** Risen Lord, you are the vine and we are your branches. May I bear the fruit of your peace, hope, compassion, and love with grace and humility.

**Practice:** Today I will bring the fruit of hope to someone who is lonely and discouraged.

# Thursday of the Fifth Week of Easter

*Acts 15:7–21*
*Psalm 96:1–2a, 2b–3, 10*
*John 15:9–11*

**Jesus answered, "As the Father has loved me, so I have loved you; abide in my love."**

JOHN 15:9

**Reflection:** Jesus shows his love for us in so many ways. He kneels to wash his disciples' feet. He heals those with leprosy so they can once again be received into society. He touches the eyes of those who are blind so they may see. He multiplies fishes and loaves to feed the hungry. He opens the ears of those who are deaf so they may hear and understand. He uses his energy, wisdom, and experience to teach the people about God's kingdom of love and peace. He comes up with numerous stories and parables to help the people understand the way to eternal love and joy. He takes self-righteous spiritual leaders to task for their treatment of the people. He brings to light the hypocrisy of those who parade their prayer life and pious actions for all to see.

Jesus makes it clear to us that love is a commitment. He teaches us that we must be intentional about bringing love with us everywhere we go. He gives us many examples of love, knowing that we each have unique gifts and talents and will bring our own individuality to our work of love.

To abide in the love of Jesus is to follow his example of love. From the place of Jesus' love, we draw the strength to move beyond our limits and practice love a little more perfectly each day. From the place of Jesus' love, we are renewed and comforted when it seems our efforts to love are rejected, ridiculed, or ignored. From the place of Jesus' love, we find the humility to place our lives and will into God's care, knowing that our attempts to love are led by the Holy Spirit.

*Ponder:* What prevents me from abiding in God's love?

*Prayer:* Risen Lord, you read our hearts from moment to moment. Cleanse me of pride and arrogance that I may learn to abide more perfectly in your love.

*Practice:* Today I will practice love.

# Friday of the Fifth Week of Easter

*Acts 15:22–31*
*Psalm 57:8–9, 10 and 12*
*John 15:12–17*

**Jesus answered, "No one has greater love than this, to lay down one's life for one's friends."**

JOHN 15:13

*Reflection:* We are deeply invested in our own world. We are committed to our work because it is a means to a successful life. We cherish our hobbies and special projects because they give meaning and purpose to our lives. We maintain a particular lifestyle and pay attention to the clothes we wear because we want to project a certain image to others. We are passionate in expressing our opinions about cultural, political, social, and religious issues only when they affect our lives. We do everything in our power to create for ourselves an orderly, comfortable world.

Yet we can be trapped in our selfish quest for success, power, and gratification. We can get swallowed up by the material world, lose our identity and the capacity to care for our family, neighbors, and friends. We can be indifferent to the sick, the oppressed, and the poor even when confronted with their pain and suffering. We can remain self-absorbed.

The resurrection, however, disturbs our comfort, changes our worldview, and liberates us from self-centeredness. The resurrection empowers us to embrace the broken human condition and to lay down our lives for the least of our brothers and sisters. During his life on earth, Jesus taught his followers to be detached from the things of the world and to live for others.

The death and resurrection of Jesus affirms God's unconditional love for all humanity. As people of the resurrection we are called to be self-giving, to love all people, to work for peace and justice, to defend life, to care for the poor, and to live a humble life. By rising from the dead, Jesus shows us that there is no greater love than to lay down one's life for one's friends.

**Ponder:** What am I willing to sacrifice for others?

**Prayer:** Risen Jesus, you offered your life as a gift to the world. Help me to be a generous friend to all people.

**Practice:** Today I will take care of another's needs before my own.

# Saturday of the Fifth Week of Easter

*Acts 16:1–10*
*Psalm 100:1b–2, 3, 5*
*John 15:18–21*

**Know that the LORD is God. It is he that made us, and we are his; we are his people, and the sheep of his pasture.**

PSALM 100:3

*Reflection:* There is such a tender bond between God and us. God is our loving creator, our father and mother, the one who knows us intimately, loves us completely, and walks always by our side.

We are God's. We are made in the image and likeness of God's love and goodness. We come from God, we dwell in God, we move with God, we grow to be more like God.

We are God's people. We populate this beautiful world to enjoy the richness and fullness of experience that life has to offer. We embody the goodness of God in our persons. We extend God's love through our care for one another. We walk in God's love and shine that love in a world that is sometimes tortured and despairing. We bring

God's reassuring hope and peace to those who feel forgotten by God.

We are the wandering, irksome, messy, crowd-following sheep in God's serene pasture of perfect love. We make mistakes. We ignore God and try to live on our own terms. We annoy one another. We become frightened. We take care of our own needs and forget the needs of others. We sign up for all that is faddish, hand over our power of decision to spiritual and political leaders, and disown our freedom to honor God's will.

God made us, and we are perfectly God's, even in our imperfection. Only God can satisfy us. Only God can understand us. Only God knows our innermost hearts. Only God can guide us, lead us, nurture us, and love us into eternity.

*Ponder:* How do I know I belong to God?

*Prayer:* Risen Lord, you made us, and we are yours. Teach me to listen to the sound of your voice that I may follow you all the days of my life.

*Practice:* Today I will read Psalm 100.

# Sixth Sunday of Easter

## YEAR A

———

*Acts 8:5–8, 14–17*
*Psalm 66:1–3, 4–5, 6–7, 16, 20*
*1 Peter 3:15–18*
*John 14:15–21*

**Jesus said, "If you love me, you will keep my commandments."**

JOHN 14:15

*Reflection:* We listen carefully to the people we have come to know, love, and respect. We listen to our parents, teachers, mentors, and close friends because they have wisdom to share with us. We can trust and learn from them because their actions match their words. We are not afraid to take their words to heart, to reflect on them, and to put them into practice.

At times, we struggle to honor the wisdom of those who have guided us, shaped our lives, and influenced our thoughts. We fail to listen to and observe what they have taught us. We know the painful consequences that follow when we betray what these wise people shared with us about faithfulness, personal responsibility, self-control, hard work, respect for others, community service, and nonviolence.

As followers of the risen Jesus, we need to listen deeply to his teachings and allow God's wisdom revealed through him to transform our minds and hearts so that our actions match God's Word. Jesus rose from the dead to empower us to live in the way of love, compassion, peace, and forgiveness.

The risen Jesus is present with us in the Word and in the Eucharist. Out of our love for the risen Jesus, we continue to gather at the eucharistic table to listen to his voice in the Word of God. We will not be afraid to accept his teachings, to reflect on them in our hearts, and to put them into practice.

There is great hope for humanity when we walk in union with the risen Jesus and observe what he commands us: Love one another.

**Ponder:** What prevents me from listening to God and keeping his commandments?

**Prayer:** Risen Lord, you remain with us and command us to love one another. Help me to show your love to all people.

**Practice:** Today I will be a living example of peace, love, compassion, and forgiveness.

# YEAR B

---

*Acts 10:25–26, 34–35, 44–48*
*Psalm 98:1, 2–3, 3–4*
*1 John 4:7–10*
*John 15:9–17*

**Beloved, let us love one another, because love is from God; everyone who loves is born of God and knows God. Whoever does not love does not know God, for God is love.**

1 JOHN 4:7–8

*Reflection:* Love is a powerful force. Love is the foundation of family life. Love brings people together and builds community. Love nurtures and sustains friendships. Love enlightens us to value life. Love moves us to show compassion to those who are suffering and in pain. Love enables us to feed the poor, to visit the sick and the imprisoned, to shelter the homeless, and to welcome the stranger. Love gives us the courage to work for peace and justice. Love humbles us to offer forgiveness to others.

When love is absent from our hearts, we feel empty, afraid, sad, and hopeless. When we refuse to love others, there is conflict and division, violence and war, racial discrimination and hatred, misery and poverty. When we withhold love from the poor, the sick, and the suffering, people die. When we fail to teach our children and youth how to love others, life is endangered.

The resurrection of Jesus is God's gift to humanity. To believe in the resurrection is to believe in God's love as the source and foundation of the universe. The risen Jesus is the living presence of God's love in the world. The universal message of the resurrection is that God's love is available to all people and that we have been given the power to love one another.

There is great hope for us and the whole world. We can overcome all obstacles with love. Believers and unbelievers alike can experience the transforming power of the resurrection and know God when we love one another.

**Ponder:** How did I come to know God?

**Prayer:** Risen Lord, you command us to love one another. Help me to show your love to all people.

**Practice:** Today I will show no partiality and will treat everyone with love.

# YEAR C

Acts 15:1–2, 22–29
Psalm 67:2–3, 5, 6, 8
Revelation 21:10–14, 22–23
John 14:23–29

Jesus answered, "But the Advocate, the Holy Spirit, whom the Father will send in my name, will teach you everything, and remind you of all that I have said to you. Peace I leave with you; my peace I give to you. I do not give to you as the world gives."

JOHN 14:26–27

**Reflection:** Memory is a precious gift. Our memory reconnects us to people and experiences that continue to give meaning to our lives. We remember the special moments shared with family members. We cherish the exciting adventures we had with childhood friends. We relive the drama of our high school years. We long for the independence and freedom we took for granted in college. We are grateful for the challenges and struggles that prepared us to be responsible, productive people.

What we remember in life influences us, grounds us, and keeps us whole. We find it easier to love others when we remember the people who loved and accepted us unconditionally. We forgive more readily when we remember the people who forgave us when we misbehaved. We are moved to befriend a stranger when we remember the people who welcomed us when we felt isolated and alone. We are more willing to console the brokenhearted when we remember the people who showed us compassion when we were suffering mental, emotional, spiritual, or physical pain.

God raised Jesus from the dead and sent us the Holy Spirit to help us remember everything Jesus taught his disciples. The resurrection reminds us that we are Jesus' followers, called to carry on his mission in the world. When we remember the risen Jesus and invite him into our lives, we can give to others what the world cannot give: love, compassion, forgiveness, hope, and peace.

*Ponder:* What are my favorite memories?

*Prayer:* Risen Lord, your death and resurrection brought peace to the world. Help me to be an instrument of your peace to others.

*Practice:* Today I will remember to be a peacemaker.

# Monday of the Sixth Week of Easter

*Acts 16:11–15*
*Psalm 149:1b–2, 3–4, 5–6a and 9b*
*John 15:26—16:4a*

**A certain woman named Lydia, a worshiper of God, was listening to us; she was from the city of Thyatira and a dealer in purple cloth. The Lord opened her heart to listen eagerly to what was said by Paul.**

ACTS 16:14

*Reflection:* Our heart is where we hear God speak. Our heart is the place of silence where God's voice reverberates. Our heart is the place of stillness where God's Word moves us to compassion and understanding. Our heart is the place of humility where God's loving presence reaffirms our dignity as precious children of God.

Our heart is always vulnerable, always innocent, always present to God. Whatever we experience in life, whatever we have stuffed, forgotten, ignored, or denied, beneath it all is a heart pure in goodness and love, ready and eager to hear God's voice of compassion, be healed by it, and go forth to share that compassion with others who have suffered.

All that we experience in life comes into our heart. When we experience rejection, sorrow, or betrayal, our heart is heavy. Our challenge is to process and let go of the heaviness, to refuse to be burdened with negative energy that may sap our spiritual strength or be the root of mental or physical illness. It takes trust in God's goodness and a willingness to embrace the fullness of life to keep our heart open to the healing touch of God's love.

Giving our experience of suffering into the healing of God's compassion makes our heart brilliant with the light of hope. Our work is to let that light go, to let it touch the people we meet, to let it warm the lives of the lonely, ill, and destitute, to let it shine hope in the darkness of selfishness, greed, and indifference.

**Ponder:** When does my heart hear God's loving voice?

**Prayer:** Risen Lord, you love me and take delight in me. Open my heart to listen eagerly to your word of hope and peace.

**Practice:** Today I will unburden my heart to a trusted friend.

# Tuesday of the Sixth Week of Easter

*Acts 16:22–34*
*Psalm 138:1–2ab, 2cde–3, 7c–8*
*John 16:5–11*

**I give you thanks, O LORD, with my whole heart.**

**PSALM 138:1**

*Reflection:* Giving thanks is an intentional act that keeps us mindful of all the good that God does for us, of all the gifts with which God blesses us, of all the experiences that come our way to teach us to be compassionate, understanding, generous, loving, and accepting.

Every day we can make a practice of finding something to give thanks for. It may be the kindness of a stranger. It may be a good night's sleep. It may be a meal someone makes for us. It may be the gift of sight or hearing. It may be the ability to walk. It may be a comfortable, safe, warm home. It may be the capacity to love and be loved.

Every day we can look at whatever is bothering us and find something to give thanks for in the situation. It may be that we are learning more patience when dealing with difficult personalities.

It may be that we are becoming more conscious of our lack of flexibility when faced with changing circumstances. It may be that we are developing awareness of our need to be right and in control of the uncontrollable.

God has given us this precious life so that we can share God's love, comfort, and compassion in the world. Every experience we have is an opportunity to let go of all that prevents us from becoming more like God in our goodness and love. Every moment of life is a call to bring the light of hope and compassion to all our experiences—positive and negative. Every breath we take is a chance to give thanks to God with our whole heart for our experiences, our blessings, and our life.

**Ponder:** For what do I give thanks to God?

**Prayer:** Risen Lord, you show me endless kindness and compassion. Give me a thankful heart that I may find your love and goodness in all that I experience.

**Practice:** Today I will give thanks to God for people or experiences in my life.

# Wednesday of the Sixth Week of Easter

*Acts 17:15, 22—18:1*
*Psalm 148:1–2, 11–12, 13, 14*
*John 16:12–15*

Then Paul said, "The God who made the world and everything in it, he who is Lord of heaven and earth, does not live in shrines made by human hands, nor is he served by human hands, as though he needed anything, since he himself gives to all mortals life and breath and all things."

ACTS 17:24–25

***Reflection:*** If God does not live in our shrines, churches, synagogues, mosques, or temples, then where do we find God?

We find God in our heart. We find God in the hearts of all people. We find God in all of creation, in all that lives and breathes, in all energetic masses. Wherever we go in the world, we find God. All of the world and all of its people are the creation of God, an expression of God's love and goodness.

We have been created to be a continual expression of God's love for the world. In places where God has been forgotten, forbidden, or forsaken, we carry the hope of God's presence. We bring comfort, encouragement, and kindness to those who are distressed and suffering. We bring consistency, faithfulness, and reliability to those who have been betrayed and abandoned. We bring respect, justice, and dignity to those who have experienced discrimination and disparagement. We bring peace, serenity, and stillness to those who are in turmoil and conflict.

Our human hands serve others so that all may be reminded of God's never-failing presence and love. Our human hands serve others so that all may be reminded that we are all God's beloved offspring, made in God's image of goodness and love. Our human hands serve others so that all will come to know and love God, who created each of us in and for love.

**Ponder:** Where do I find God?

**Prayer:** Risen Lord, you guide me in truth and love. Help me to willingly serve your people so that all may know your goodness and love.

**Practice:** Today I will lend a helping hand to someone in need.

# Thursday of the Sixth Week of Easter

*Acts 18:1–8*
*Psalm 98:1, 2–3ab, 3cd–4*
*John 16:16–20*

After this Paul left Athens and went to Corinth. There he found a Jew named Aquila, a native of Pontus, who had recently come from Italy with his wife Priscilla, because Claudius had ordered all Jews to leave Rome.

ACTS 18:1–2

*Reflection:* Aquila and Priscilla remind us that Jesus comes from a race of people who have been expelled from their lands, chased from their homes, and persecuted to death. During his life, Jesus also experienced the pain of rejection, displacement, and loneliness yet remained faithful to completing God's work on earth.

Jesus lived in a society in which challenging the complacency and conformity of the people was personally dangerous. His mission to teach the unconditional love and mercy of God marked him as a rebel. His presence was perceived as a threat to those in power. His countercultural message of love, peace, and forgiveness was not always accepted. Even his followers misunderstood him and betrayed him.

Jesus understands the frustration of being the peacemaker in a place of conflict. He understands the emotional isolation of being the one who points the way to forgiveness and reconciliation in the face of resentment and blame. He understands the loneliness of being the one who lives simply in a world of self-indulgence, who cares deeply in a world of indifference, who has a vision of unity in a world divided by prejudice, fear, and greed.

In all that we experience, Jesus identifies with us personally—at the level of our suffering, at the level of our human frailty, and at the level of our power to love, heal, and carry the good news of God's compassion and forgiveness.

**Ponder:** When has suffering deepened my relationship with Jesus?

**Prayer:** Risen Lord, you walk with me every step of my day. Help me to see you in all of my sisters and brothers and to pledge my energy to the work of healing, peace, and reconciliation.

**Practice:** Today I will support an organization that finds homes for displaced persons and refugees.

# Friday of the Sixth Week of Easter

*Acts 18:9–18*
*Psalm 47:2–3, 4–5, 6–7*
*John 16:20–23*

**One night the Lord said to Paul in a vision, "Do not be afraid, but speak and do not be silent; for I am with you, and no one will lay a hand on you to harm you, for there are many in this city who are my people."**

ACTS 18:9–10

**Reflection:** Again and again in sacred Scripture we hear, "Do not be afraid." Again and again we are reminded that God is with us. Our faith tells us that with God by our side, nothing can harm us. Yet we continue to feel afraid and often let that fear control our thoughts, actions, and words.

Being afraid can become a habit. Sometimes we are afraid of making others angry by saying what is in our hearts. Sometimes we are afraid of being hurt if we love someone or let someone love us. Sometimes we are afraid of losing our job if we take a stand against something we feel is wrong or unjust. Sometimes we are afraid of getting old, getting sick, being dependent on others, or being alone.

Overcoming fear takes a commitment on our part, but it can be done. We are greater than fear.

Awareness is our greatest ally in overcoming fear. When we are aware of the fear, we can name it, describe it, and look at the reasons for our fear. We ask God to be right by our side to show us how to address and banish the fear.

Letting go of fear is a skill we learn with practice. Each day we can ask God to show us our fears and help us overcome them. Each day we can trust that God is by our side, leading us gently on the path of love, helping us to leave all fear behind.

**Ponder:** What do I fear?

**Prayer:** Risen Lord, you are always with me. Help me to love more and fear less.

**Practice:** Today I will refuse to be controlled by fear.

# Saturday of the Sixth Week of Easter

*Acts 18:23–28*
*Psalm 47:2–3, 8–9, 10*
*John 16:23b–28*

**Jesus said, "Until now you have not asked for anything in my name. Ask and you will receive, so that your joy may be complete."**

JOHN 16:24

*Reflection:* What makes it so hard to ask for what we want or need? What prevents us from sharing our longings, desires, and hopes with God, who loves us so completely?

We have been told so often that we are unworthy that we tend to believe it. We have been reminded so often not to be self-centered that we tend to suppress our needs. We have been admonished so often to serve the needs of others that we tend to forget that Jesus told us to love our neighbor as ourselves.

If we do not love ourselves; if we do not accept our human needs, weaknesses, and shortcomings; if we do not recognize our human dignity and worth; if we do not examine our lives to discern our passions, strengths, and talents—then we are neglecting ourselves. We need to know the all of ourselves to do the work of God. We need to be fearless in our exploration of who we are, what fulfills us, what prevents us from trusting ourselves, what keeps us from embodying the hope and peace of God, and what we need to give and receive love.

We need to learn to be fearless in our relationship with God. God will never hurt us. God will always give us what we need. God will provide everything we need to move through difficult times, to bear unbearable burdens, to use our gifts and talents in ways that bring hope to the world. We have been given the freedom to ask and ask and ask again so that God may have the joy of fulfilling our needs.

*Ponder:* What do I need to ask of God?

*Prayer:* Risen Lord, you have come from God the Father in love. Give me the courage to ask God in your name of love for what I need today.

*Practice:* Today I will trust God to provide everything I need for the day.

# The Ascension of the Lord

## YEAR A

---

*Acts 1:1–11*
*Psalm 47:2–3, 6–7, 8–9*
*Ephesians 1:17–23*
*Matthew 28:16–20*

Jesus said, "Go therefore and make disciples of all nations, baptizing them in the name of the Father and of the Son and of the Holy Spirit, and teaching them to obey everything that I have commanded you. And remember, I am with you always, to the end of the age."

MATTHEW 28:19–20

*Reflection:* We all have a special calling or mission in life. We are drawn to a way of life that gives us a sense of purpose. Some people feel called to raise a family, to become an educator, a social worker, an engineer, a scientist, a doctor, a nurse, a lawyer, an electrician, a carpenter, a law enforcement officer, an accountant, a politician, a spiritual leader, a musician, or an artist.

It takes time to discern our calling in life. We need to observe and work with others to get a sense of what we would like to become. Our calling in life is not about ourselves; it is connected to a universal vision of a world in which all people can live and work together in love and peace. Inherent in our calling is a common desire to serve people, to improve the quality of life, and to teach others what we have learned.

After Jesus rose from the dead and before he ascended into heaven, he gave his disciples a mission to carry out. Their mission was to be a sign of Jesus' presence in the world, to gather people together into one family, and to teach them how to love one another. At baptism, we received the same mission. God's mission must be reflected in our lives and in our work. We have been called in the risen Jesus to be God's presence, to build community, to love and serve others.

**Ponder:** What is my mission in life?

**Prayer:** Risen Lord, you share with us the mission of God. Help me to use my gifts and talents to do God's work.

**Practice:** Today I will make God's work my own.

# YEAR B

---

*Acts 1:1–11*
*Psalm 47:2–3, 6–7, 8–9*
*Ephesians 1:17–23 or 4:1–13 or 4:1–7, 11–13*
*Mark 16:15–20*

**[Jesus] said to them, "Go into all the world and proclaim the good news to the whole creation."**

**MARK 16:15**

***Reflection:*** We are constantly on the move. We are always getting into a car to go somewhere. We go to work to earn a living and to school to earn a degree. We go to the supermarket to buy food and to the mall to buy clothing. We go to the doctor for physical checkups. We go to the fitness center to work out. We go to the movies, the theater, restaurants, or the casino to be entertained. We go to the parks, the mountains, the lakes, the rivers, and the ocean to relax. Our personal priorities in life are reflected in the places we go.

We seldom find ourselves going to a hospital or nursing home to visit the sick and the elderly. We do not go to see the neighbor next-door. We do not schedule time to go to a soup kitchen to prepare and serve a meal to the poor. We are not inclined to go to the jail to visit an inmate. We struggle to go to church to praise and thank God for being so good to us. We are not interested in going to Bible study or to a prayer meeting or to adult-formation classes to deepen our relationship with God. We find it difficult to go to places where we have to give of ourselves.

We are free to go wherever we desire, but wherever we go, Jesus instructs us to go with "the good news" of God in our hearts. We are called to show everyone we meet the love, compassion, peace, and goodness of God.

**Ponder:** How do I live the gospel in my life?

**Prayer:** Risen Lord, your death, resurrection, and ascension are good news for us. Help me to share this message of hope with all people.

**Practice:** Today I will think about God before I go anywhere.

# YEAR C

---

*Acts 1:1–11*
*Psalm 47:2–3, 6–7, 8–9*
*Ephesians 1:17–23 or Hebrews 9:24–28; 10:19–23*
*Luke 24:46–53*

[Jesus] said to them, "Thus it is written, that the Messiah is to suffer and to rise from the dead on the third day, and that repentance and forgiveness of sins is to be proclaimed in his name to all nations, beginning from Jerusalem. You are witnesses of these things."

LUKE 24:46–48

***Reflection:*** We cannot keep secret some experiences in life. The miraculous birth of a newborn child, the beautiful marriage of dear friends, a joyous graduation ceremony, a breathtaking sunrise or sunset, a powerful earthquake, a moving play, an outstanding concert performance, a spectacular sports event, and a significant personal achievement are some of the unique, life-changing experiences we want to share with others.

Our personal encounter with the risen Jesus is also a life-changing experience. It is too extraordinary to be kept private. Our belief in the resurrection of Jesus keeps our lives open to the transforming power of God's love, compassion, forgiveness, and peace. Every day we have an opportunity for an ongoing, life-changing experience when we encounter the risen Jesus in the prayerful reading of the Scriptures and in serving the needs of the poor.

We need to share the joy and excitement of our experience of the risen Jesus with others. We can begin by not being afraid to share with others how our faith and our love of the Lord influence our words and actions. We can gently invite people to read and reflect on the gospels with us, to worship and pray with us, and to join us in doing works of charity. We have to practice what we preach before others find us to be authentic witnesses.

**Ponder:** Why am I afraid to share my faith with others?

**Prayer:** Risen Lord, your resurrection and ascension give witness to God's power. May my life bear witness to God's love, compassion, forgiveness, and peace.

**Practice:** Today I will be open to an opportunity to share my faith with others.

# Seventh Sunday of Easter

## YEAR A

---

*Acts 1:12–14*
*Psalm 27:1, 4, 7–8*
*1 Peter 4:13–16*
*John 17:1–11a*

**[Jesus] looked up to heaven and said, "I am asking on their behalf; I am not asking on behalf of the world, but on behalf of those whom you gave me, because they are yours. All mine are yours, and yours are mine; and I have been glorified in them."**

JOHN 17:1, 9–10

***Reflection:*** We are all caught up in the human condition. We know the frailty of the human condition whenever we experience mental anguish, emotional hurt, spiritual confusion, and physical pain. There are moments along the journey of life when we feel powerless, afraid, vulnerable, and alone. We want a compassionate, unselfish person to notice us, to reach out to us and help us.

We are also members of a global family. We live in solidarity with people from various cultures, tribes, and villages. Our lives are affected when we see people suffering from famine, drought, natural disasters, disease, torture, violence, and war. These tragic realities put our selfishness in check and challenge us to share what we have. Our hearts are moved to intercede on behalf of all the poor and helpless people throughout the world.

During his life on earth, Jesus was a man of prayer. He taught his disciples how to be humble, prayerful servants of God. In prayer, he showed them how to bring the frail human condition and the human family into communion with God. For Jesus, prayer was a selfless act of love, offered on behalf of others.

As Christians we worship the crucified and risen Jesus who intercedes for us. When we dare to pray as Jesus did, we bring the frail human condition and the human family into communion with God. We let the poor and suffering know that we notice them and care. In prayer, we become like the crucified and risen Jesus who prayed on behalf of others.

**Ponder:** Why do I pray?

**Prayer:** Risen Lord, your life was a prayer to God. Help me to live a prayerful life.

**Practice:** Today I will spend extra time in prayer.

# YEAR B

———

*Acts 1:15–17, 20a, 20c–26*
*Psalm 103:1–2, 11–12, 19–20*
*1 John 4:11–16*
*John 17:11b–19*

**No one has ever seen God; if we love one another, God lives in us, and his love is perfected in us. By this we know that we abide in him and he in us, because he has given us of his Spirit.**

1 JOHN 4:12–13

***Reflection:*** We experience the church as a sacred place where God abides. It is a special place set apart from the chaos of the world where we can be in communion with God. We enter the quiet space to pray to God for our family and friends, for the sick and the poor, and for all the suffering people throughout the world. Though we cannot see God, we can encounter God and feel God's Spirit within us.

We find it more difficult to believe that God abides in our hearts. Our hearts, too, are sacred places where God abides. We can sit in the quiet of our hearts to commune with God, to experience God, and to feel God's Spirit in us. Within our hearts we can savor the Word of God. Within our hearts, we can pray to God for the needs of others, for compassion, forgiveness, healing, and peace. Though we cannot see God, we sense God's presence in us.

We know that God is love and that God's preferred dwelling place is in our hearts. Even though the world cannot see God, we reveal God's presence when we love one another. After Jesus rose and ascended into heaven, God's Spirit was sent to dwell in the hearts of the disciples. We have the Spirit of God's love in us. When we love one another, God's love fills the world and transforms the hearts of all people.

*Ponder:* When do I experience the Spirit of God's love?

*Prayer:* Risen Lord, you abide in our hearts. Help me to make a home for you in my heart.

*Practice:* Today I will dwell in my heart and not in the world.

# YEAR C

---

*Acts 7:55–60*
*Psalm 97:1–2, 6–7, 9*
*Revelation 22:12–14, 16–17, 20*
*John 17:20–26*

> Jesus said, "Righteous Father, the world does not know you, but I know you; and these know that you have sent me. I made your name known to them, and I will make it known, so that the love with which you have loved me may be in them, and I in them."
>
> JOHN 17:25–26

*Reflection:* Love is the source and foundation of life. It is in our nature to love and be loved by others. Our purpose in the world is to share love with others and to help everyone understand that all people—regardless of their race, color, culture, language, religious belief, or way of life—are lovable. Love is the energy that brings us together and makes us one family.

Since we all share in a common, universal love, each of us possesses a common dignity. We are intimately connected to every person on this earth. Love motivates us to see what we share in common, helps us to appreciate our differences, and inspires us to live in harmony with others. Love is the universal principle that orders our relationships and activities toward the common good.

When our thoughts, feelings, and actions are not grounded in love, we convey to others a message that goes against our nature. It is unnatural for us to abuse people, to be violent, to create war, to disrespect others, and to destroy life. When we distrust our instinct for love and goodness, we open the door for unspeakable crimes to be committed against humanity.

God's love is revealed through the death and resurrection of Jesus. We have been given a share in the Spirit of the risen Jesus so that we may continue to make known in the world the healing, transforming power of God's love and compassion.

*Ponder:* How do I share God's love?

*Prayer:* Risen Lord, you are God's gift of unconditional love. Empower me to be this gift to all people.

*Practice:* Today I will show God's love in thought, word, and deed.

# Monday of the Seventh Week of Easter

*Acts 19:1–8*
*Psalm 68:2–3ab, 4–5acd, 6–7ab*
*John 16:29–33*

**Jesus answered them, "Yet I am not alone because the Father is with me."**

**JOHN 16:32**

***Reflection:*** Jesus reassures us that being alone is not possible because God is always with us. We are always with and in the community of God. The Holy Trinity is our source of companionship, hope, and love.

In our human lives, there are times of loneliness. We experience the loneliness of grief when a loved one dies. No one else can process our grief; we alone must wrestle with the feelings of loss, anger, and depression. We experience the loneliness of moving away from family, friends, and all that is familiar. No one else can process our feelings of being without roots; we must find a way to make new connections for ourselves. We experience the loneliness of living alone with no one to help with chores, decisions, or finances. No one else can assume our responsibilities; we must rely on our own creativity to balance all that we need for a healthy, fulfilling life.

While we must do our own work, God is always with us—in our hearts, in the presence of others, in the beauties of the natural world, in the prayers of those who care about us. However lonely we might feel, we are never bereft, we are never alone.

When we feel lonely, we have simply forgotten our deep, personal connection to God. A sure cure for loneliness is to sit quietly and become present to God in the stillness. Sometimes we are afraid of the stillness. We worry that it is empty and we will feel even more lonely. Yet if we persevere, listening for the voice of God in the peace of our hearts, we will feel God's compassionate presence and find hope and comfort.

We are never alone. God is always with us.

**Ponder:** What happens when I feel lonely?

**Prayer:** Risen Lord, in you I find my peace. Remind me to turn to you when I feel lost and lonely.

**Practice:** Today I will visit someone who lives alone.

# Tuesday of the Seventh Week of Easter

*Acts 20:17–27*
*Psalm 68:10–11, 20–21*
*John 17:1–11a*

**Jesus said, "And this is eternal life, that they may know you, the only true God, and Jesus Christ whom you have sent."**

JOHN 17:3

*Reflection:* To know God, to know Jesus, to know them in our hearts, through our lives, with every word, thought, emotion, and action: This is eternal life, eternal love. Eternal life within the community of God is ever aware, ever loving, ever embracing of all people everywhere.

Knowing is being aware. Awareness of God with every breath, in every moment: This is eternal life, life lived in conscious contact with God who is love, who created us in love and for love.

Being aware is being responsible. Responsible for choosing to live in God, to live the way of love, hope, peace, and compassion. Responsible for our interactions with others, showing respect, sharing generously, helping those in need, feeding those who are hungry, finding homes for those who are homeless, visiting those who are lonely and afraid. Responsible for ourselves, for the choices we make, the companions we select, the way we spend our time, the way we use the earth's resources, the way we speak to others, the way we respond to those in need. Responsible for every kind word, every loving gesture, every act of selfishness or indifference. Responsible for how we use the gifts and talents we have been given. Responsible for our willingness to hear and respond to the Word of God.

We come to know God through the life of Jesus. We see the compassion of Jesus, his humble acceptance of God's will, his deep prayer life, his healing of the sick, his welcome of those who are social outcasts. Hoping to know God more truly, we seek to be more aware of the gift of life, to be responsible for how we live this precious gift.

*Ponder:* Do I know God?

*Prayer:* Risen Lord, you bear our burdens and bless our days. Help me to know you and share your love with everyone I encounter.

*Practice:* Today I will take responsibility for treating everyone I encounter with kindness.

# Wednesday of the Seventh Week of Easter

*Acts 20:28–38*
*Psalm 68:29–30, 33–35a, 35bc–36ab*
*John 17:11b–19*

**Paul said to them, "Keep watch over yourselves and over all the flock, of which the Holy Spirit has made you overseers."**

*Reflection:* By the grace of God, in the name of Jesus, and through the power of the Holy Spirit, we have been called to watch over one another. We have been called to love one another, to forgive our enemies, to help the poor, and to heal the sick. We have been called to cherish the lives of all people, regardless of culture, race, age, gender, sexual orientation, or social status. We have been called to reach out in compassion to bring hope and support to those in need. We have been called to do the work of God—the work of reconciliation, peace, unity, and love—throughout the world for the flock that is humanity, the flock of the people of God.

We keep watch over ourselves by taking time to read and reflect on the Word of God in sacred

Scripture. We keep watch over ourselves by finding a quiet space where we can pray and come to know God more deeply. We keep watch over ourselves by resting when we are tired, eating when we are hungry, talking through our difficulties with trusted friends, and seeking God's presence in our hearts and in the company of others.

We keep watch over others by our willingness to love and accept all people unconditionally. We keep watch over others by encouraging creativity, vision, and resourcefulness. We keep watch over others by being a caring, compassionate, and hopeful presence.

The Holy Spirit fills us with the power and love to answer the call to watch over ourselves and all of the human flock. The Holy Spirit is our guide and inspiration as we perform God's work of love and hope in the world.

**Ponder:** How do I tend the flock of God's people?

**Prayer:** Risen Lord, you give me power and strength through your Holy Spirit. Show me how to watch over your flock with compassion and acceptance.

**Practice:** Today I will watch over someone who needs encouragement and support.

# Thursday of the Seventh Week of Easter

*Acts 22:30; 23:6–11*
*Psalm 16:1–2a and 5, 7–8, 9–10, 11*
*John 17:20–26*

> Jesus said, "The glory that you have given me I have given them, so that they may be one, as we are one, I in them and you in me, that they may become completely one, so that the world may know that you have sent me and have loved them even as you have loved me."
>
> JOHN 17:22–23

**Reflection:** Jesus offers us a vision of unity, a vision where all people are one in love and peace. Jesus teaches us to embrace this vision and to rejoice in the glory of God dwelling in us. Jesus shows us how each of us is entwined with God, with the superabundant love of God as our source of life, power, and goodness.

Jesus, God-with-us, pours out his life and love on our behalf so that we might join in the harmonious union that is the community of God. The Holy Spirit fills our hearts with courage, humility, and willingness so that we dare to make our lives a reflection of God's love and healing presence in the world.

Jesus, the compassion of God, kneels at our feet to wash them, reaches out to heal the sick and broken, stays grounded in God's love in the face of adversity, and seeks God's will at every stage of his mission to bring the good news of God's love and forgiveness to humankind. Jesus, the Prince of Peace, commands us to abandon our way of war, violence, and greed and, instead, to adopt the way of mercy, reconciliation, and generosity. Jesus, the Bread of Life, feeds us with his example of service, prayer, and friendship so that we may be sustained as we carry on the mission to encourage love and unity among all God's people.

**Ponder:** How do I show the world the glory of God's love?

**Prayer:** Risen Lord, you are the glory of unity, harmony, and everlasting peace. Help me to carry your love and compassion wherever I go.

**Practice:** Today I will stay mindful of God's presence in me and in all of my sisters and brothers.

# Friday of the
# Seventh Week of Easter

*Acts 25:13b–21*
*Psalm 103:1–2, 11–12, 19–20ab*
*John 21:15–19*

**Jesus said to [Peter], "Feed my sheep."**

JOHN 21:17

*Reflection:* Life is good! We do not have to worry about being without clean water to drink, food to eat, clothing to wear, a nice home to live in, a mode of transportation, many opportunities to learn, and a chance to engage in meaningful work. When we become sick, we can go to a hospital to receive care. We are guilty of taking for granted many of the perks that sustain our comfortable lifestyle.

It is hard to imagine that life is not so good for millions of people throughout the world who are near death because they have no clean water to drink, no food to eat, no clothes to wear, no shelter for their families, no mode of transportation, no opportunity to learn, no chance to engage in meaningful work, no hospitals to go to when they are sick, and no way out of their miserable human condition.

We can become insulated in our own world, disconnected from others, unaware of the poor, and unresponsive to their needs. Our inability to show love and care to others is a sign of a disordered life, a life turned in on our own selfish needs. Life is good when we turn our hearts in love toward God and neighbor.

The words of Jesus—"Feed my sheep"—challenge us to make life better for the least of our brothers and sisters. His instruction is meant to disturb and move us out of our comfort zone. Our love for the risen Jesus is actualized when we feed the hungry, clothe the naked, shelter the homeless, care for the sick, and advocate for those oppressed and deprived of freedom.

**Ponder:** What do I need to do to tend and feed God's sheep?

**Prayer:** Risen Lord, you have called us to tend and feed your sheep. Help me to imitate your love and feed the poor.

**Practice:** Today I will bring a bag of canned goods to a food pantry.

# Saturday of the Seventh Week of Easter

*Acts 28:16–20, 30–31*
*Psalm 11:4, 5 and 7*
*John 21:20–25*

[Paul] welcomed all who came to him, pro-claiming the kingdom of God and teaching about the Lord Jesus Christ with all boldness and without hindrance.

ACTS 28:30–31

**Reflection:** Hospitality is an act of kindness extended to a stranger. Yet we have been conditioned by the secular world to see the stranger as a threat to our way of life, security, and peace. Before we can extend hospitality to a stranger, we need to overcome our fears and prejudices of people from different racial, cultural, ethnic, and social backgrounds.

When we open our hearts and welcome a stranger into our lives, we make the person feel at home. When we acknowledge and accept the stranger as a member of the human family, we affirm the truth that every person deserves respect, has innate value and dignity.

When we invite a stranger to sit at table and eat with us, we build community. When we have a conversation with a stranger, we remove barriers and foster peace. When we share our resources with a stranger, we help to eradicate poverty in the world.

When Jesus rose from the dead, he walked among his disciples as a stranger. With love and tenderness, Jesus welcomed them, accepted them, and made them feel at home. By his example, Jesus taught his disciples that hospitality is the hallmark of Christian discipleship. When we welcome a stranger, we welcome the risen Jesus into our hearts.

When we practice hospitality, we make present God's kingdom of love, compassion, forgiveness, justice, and peace. Empowered by God's Spirit, we are able to welcome all people as our brothers and sisters. When we offer hospitality to others, we hope to be treated the way we have treated others.

**Ponder:** Why do I find it difficult to welcome strangers into my life?

**Prayer:** Risen Lord, you walk among us as a stranger. Open my eyes to recognize your presence in all the strangers I meet.

**Practice:** Today I will not avoid a stranger. I will be pleasant and welcoming to all people.

# Pentecost Sunday—Vigil

## YEARS A, B, AND C

---

*Genesis 11:1–9 or Exodus 19:3–8a, 16–20b
or Ezekiel 37:1–14 or Joel 3:1–5
Psalm 104:1–2, 24, 35, 27–28, 29, 30
Romans 8:22–27
John 7:37–39*

**Likewise the Spirit helps us in our weakness; for we do not know how to pray as we ought, but that very Spirit intercedes with sighs too deep for words. And God, who searches the heart, knows what is the mind of the Spirit, because the Spirit intercedes for the saints according to the will of God.**

ROMANS 8:26–27

*Reflection:* Sometimes we are afraid to admit that we are overwhelmed, that life is not easy, that we are mentally burdened, emotionally unavailable, spiritually dry, and physically drained. We try to mask our brokenness and pain. We do not want to appear helpless, needy, or weak. In public, we pretend we have everything under control and can make it on our own. In the privacy of our homes, we fall apart and cry.

Sometimes the pain is so unbearable that we cannot find words to describe what we are going through. It hurts too much to think and feel. The inner struggle to find meaning and purpose for our suffering is fruitless. No matter what we do to numb the pain, we experience no relief from all the hurts and wounds that we have carried in our hearts, minds, and bodies.

Deep within us, God's Spirit is attentive to what afflicts us, interceding for us, asking God to come to our aid. God's Spirit searches our hearts. God's Spirit knows what we need to have peace and to be whole again. God's Spirit raises us from the depths of despair, gives us hope, and renews our lives with the love of God. When we find ourselves in a dark, unknown place, God's Spirit intercedes for us.

**Ponder:** What weakness do I hide from others?

**Prayer:** Risen Lord, you send us your Spirit to renew our lives and the face of this earth. Help me to trust your Spirit to renew and strengthen me when I am in trouble.

**Practice:** Today I will trust that all will be well.

# Pentecost Sunday

## YEAR A

---

*Acts 2:1–11*
*Psalm 104:1, 24, 29–30, 31, 34*
*1 Corinthians 12:3b–7, 12–13*
*John 20:19–23*

Jesus said to them, "Receive the Holy Spirit. If you forgive the sins of any, they are forgiven them; if you retain the sins of any, they are retained."

JOHN 20:22–23

*Reflection:* We need to be aware that our words have power. Our words are a window into our inner world; they offer insight into what we believe and how we feel about life. With our words we influence people's lives. Our words create a moral vision of life, give meaning to our human existence, articulate basic principles, promote goodness, and support the dignity of all people.

Our actions also have power. Our actions often speak louder than our words. We reveal who we are through our actions. We are love when we embrace people from different races, cultures, traditions, and social conditions. We are compassion when we attend to the needs of others, visit the sick, feed the poor, clothe the naked, and shelter the homeless. We are nonviolence when we promote peace and justice and advocate for refugees and the oppressed.

We confuse people when our actions and words are inconsistent. We cause despair when we remain silent in the face of hunger, famine, and the destruction of life. We are not good role models for our children and youth when our actions promote abuse, hatred, and violence toward others.

We have received the gift of God's Spirit. Our words and actions are empowered by God's Spirit of love, compassion, peace, and forgiveness. God's will is reflected in our words and actions when we allow God's Spirit to work in and through us. With God's Spirit, we have countless opportunities to forgive and love one another, to be peacemakers, and to renew the face of the earth.

*Ponder:* How do I cooperate with the Spirit of God?

*Prayer:* Risen Lord, your Spirit fills the world with love and peace. Empower me to be an instrument of your peace, love, and forgiveness to all people.

*Practice:* Today I will say "I am sorry" when I have hurt others.

# YEAR B

———

*Acts 2:1–11*
*Psalm 104:1, 24, 29–30, 31, 34*
*1 Corinthians 12:3b–7, 12–13*
*or Galatians 5:16–25*
*John 20:19–23 or 15:26–27; 16:12–15*

"All that the Father has is mine. For this reason I said that he will take what is mine and declare it to you."

JOHN 16:15

*Reflection:* We know love because our parents cared for us and shared their love with us. We know goodness because we had people in our lives who shared good experiences with us. We know compassion because we had friends who stood by us and walked with us through the difficult, turbulent times of life. We know forgiveness because there were people who believed in us, took a risk, and gave us another chance. We have knowledge and wisdom because we had selfless teachers and mentors who instructed and guided us. We can live with hope in our hearts because we are surrounded by a supportive, life-nurturing community.

Our world is filled with children and youth who do not know love because no one ever shared their love with them. Countless poor and homeless people remain invisible in our communities; they do not feel good about themselves because no one ever told them they were good. Many undocumented immigrants live in fear and feel like strangers in a foreign land because no one ever made them feel welcome. People from all walks of life suffer from loneliness and depression because no one has time to give them a listening ear. We need to be more aware of the fragile and wounded people around us waiting to become members of a compassionate, loving community.

Pentecost reminds us that all of creation and humanity have been filled with everything that belongs to God. We cannot keep the gifts of God to ourselves. We have been empowered with the Spirit of God to make known to all people what God has already given us: goodness, love, compassion, peace, and forgiveness. When we share with others what God has given us, we give people hope, renew life, foster peace, and bring people into the universal family of humankind.

*Ponder:* What gifts am I withholding from others?

*Prayer:* Lord, your Spirit renews our faith, hope, and love. Empower me to be your presence of love and compassion to others.

*Practice:* Today I will be a hopeful presence to someone in need.

# YEAR C

---

*Acts 2:1–11*

*Psalm 104:1, 24, 29–30, 31, 34*

*1 Corinthians 12:3b–7, 12–13 or Romans 8:8–17*

*John 20:19–23 or 14:15–16, 23b–26*

**But you are not in the flesh; you are in the Spirit, since the Spirit of God dwells in you.**

ROMANS 8:9

**Reflection:** God's Spirit dwells within us to guide and inspire us as we make our way through life. God's Spirit gives us courage to face life's challenges with dignity and good humor. God's Spirit gives us wisdom to discern a path of peace, love, and compassion in the midst of conflicts, fear, and narcissism. God's Spirit gives us hope in God's goodness and inspires us to look for that same goodness in our sisters and brothers.

God's Spirit is greater than any weakness or frailty that can assault our human flesh. When we suffer from chronic illness, it is God's Spirit that lifts us out of self-centered preoccupation to reach out in compassion to others who are suffering. When we are grief-stricken from the death of a loved one, it is God's Spirit that leads us to a place of acceptance and healing. When we succumb to addiction, deceit, or betrayal, it is God's Spirit that brings us to our senses and to our knees in genuine contrition.

God's Spirit leads us beyond our human limitations so that we become more patient, kind, understanding, and gentle with those we encounter in our daily lives. God's Spirit infuses us with creative love that we learn to express in speaking, listening, writing, artwork, cooking, and craftsmanship. God's Spirit guides us to be awed by the beauty of the natural world, the exquisite precision with which the world and universe function, and the complete interdependence of all the parts that make us the whole of God's creation.

God's Spirit within us is a holy energy, the breath of God, a gift that has been freely and generously bestowed on us, God's beloved children.

**Ponder:** How do I let God's Spirit guide me throughout the day?

**Prayer:** Lord, you send forth your Spirit. Teach me to walk your way of love and compassion in hope and gratitude.

**Practice:** Today I will ask God's Spirit within me to show me what to do and how to do it.

# Feast Days

# Solemnity of the Most Holy Trinity

## YEAR A

---

*Exodus 34:4b–6, 8–9*
*Daniel 3:52, 53, 54, 55*
*2 Corinthians 13:11–13*
*John 3:16–18*

**The grace of the Lord Jesus Christ, the love of God, and the communion of the Holy Spirit be with all of you.**

2 CORINTHIANS 13:13

*Reflection:* We carry within us the genetic makeup of our parents that was passed on to us at birth. We have within us some of our parents' features, facial makeup, intelligence, gifts, talents, and behaviors. We share things in common with the members of our family because we are connected to a family tree.

The Holy Trinity is the DNA of the Christian life. We have been imprinted with the divine life and love of the Triune God. We have within our nature the instinct of the Trinity: the instinct to love, share peace, create family, and live in communion with others. We do not reflect often enough on our divine origin, yet we need to pay attention to this God instinct in us and use our creative imagination to fashion our lives in the likeness of the Triune God.

In these challenging times, when people are divided against one another because of race, language, culture, tribe, nationality, and religious belief, we must remember that we come from the community of God in which there is eternal unity, peace, and love. God has given us everything we need to bring about unity, peace, and love in the world.

As Christians we have a unique calling and obligation to resemble the life of the Trinity in the world. This means making an effort to align our thoughts with the wisdom of God, to form our hearts with the love of Jesus, and to unite our souls with the Spirit of God. Our mission in life is to carry out the Trinity's mission of bringing together all people into one human family.

*Ponder:* What does my life look like in the Trinity?

*Prayer:* Lord, you live in communion with God and the Holy Spirit. Help me to live in communion and peace with all people.

*Practice:* Today I will strive to be in harmony with everyone I encounter.

# YEAR B

————

*Deuteronomy 4:32–34, 39–40*
*Psalm 33:4–5, 6, 9, 18–19, 20, 22*
*Romans 8:14–17*
*Matthew 28:16–20*

Jesus said to them, "Go therefore and make disciples of all nations, baptizing them in the name of the Father and of the Son and of the Holy Spirit, and teaching them to obey everything that I have commanded you. And remember, I am with you always, to the end of the age."

MATTHEW 28:19–20

*Reflection:* Wherever we go, the Triune God is with us. If we remember this truth as we journey through life, we can be more faithful witnesses to the gift of love that comes forth from the Trinity.

In the life of the Triune God there is no division, no conflict, no tension, no violence, no war, and no inequality. When we reflect deeply on the inner nature of the Trinity, we begin to see our own nature and the mission that has been entrusted to us. Our life is with the Triune God. We must do our best to live in the world from within the community of

God. When we are grounded in this reality, our life and relationships will begin to look like the inner life of the Trinity.

Strengthened by the grace of God, we are capable of doing what Jesus has commanded us to do: love one another as God has loved us. We are collaborators with the Trinity. We have been entrusted with the mission of building up the kingdom of God on earth by bringing people into the life of the Trinity.

People will know that God is with us when we inspire them to love all people, to serve the poor, and to uphold the sanctity of life. As Christians, we have been commissioned to do our part to share our faith in God, to teach and to live, as Jesus did, in peace and communion with all people.

**Ponder:** What has God commissioned me to do with my life?

**Prayer:** Lord, you command me to love all people. Remove the prejudice that keeps me from loving my brothers and sisters.

**Practice:** Today I will spend time with someone I have neglected.

# YEAR C

---

*Proverbs 8:22–31*
*Psalm 8:4–5, 6–7, 8–9*
*Romans 5:1–5*
*John 16:12–15*

**Jesus said, "All that the Father has is mine. For this reason I said that he will take what is mine and declare it to you."**

JOHN 16:15

*Reflection:* There can be no true act of love, no pure gift of self if we are holding something back. True love always involves self-sacrifice. The Triune God is always caught up in the act of total love and pure self-sacrifice.

God holds nothing back. All that God possesses is poured out to us and for us in Jesus. There is no selfishness to be found in God; there is only self-giving. Everything we need to live a good life is found in God's gift of self in Jesus. Our faith in Jesus gives us access to the gifts of God: unconditional love, compassion, and peace.

Our life in God means a life of self-giving, a life for others, and a life of humble service. In the gospels, Jesus reveals the vision of the kingdom of God. Through Jesus, God shows us how to live an authentic human life. Through Jesus, God tells us unambiguously to love one another, forgive one another, and be reconciled with our brothers and sisters.

Through Jesus, God urges us to look beyond ourselves, beyond our own needs, and to take care of the poor in our midst. Through Jesus, God opens a way for us to experience a bit of eternity on earth.

The fundamental message of God in and through Jesus is one of selfless love. God's will is that we share generously what we have and not withhold the gifts of love, compassion, peace, and forgiveness from anyone. God teaches us through the life of Jesus that anything that diminishes the life and dignity of the human person is contrary to the wisdom of God.

**Ponder:** What am I holding back from others?

**Prayer:** Lord, you willingly gave up your life for the salvation of the world. Give me the courage to love freely and unconditionally.

**Practice:** Today I will pray for the members of my family and tell them I love them.

# Solemnity of the Most Holy Body and Blood of Christ

## YEAR A

---

*Deuteronomy 8:2–3, 14b–16a*
*Psalm 147:12–13, 14–15, 19–20*
*1 Corinthians 10:16–17*
*John 6:51–58*

**Because there is one bread, we who are many are one body, for we all partake of the one bread.**

**1 CORINTHIANS 10:17**

*Reflection:* What is a home without a table? The table is the place where members of the family gather to give thanks to God for the many blessings of life, to eat a meal together, to share old and new stories, to ponder the deep questions of life, and to simply enjoy one another's presence. The table creates bonds of love and friendship and community. When we gather to eat and drink around a table, we willingly participate in the drama of the human condition.

What is the church without a table? The table is the place where we gather to give praise and thanks to the Triune God through whom all things were made. We gather to listen to the Word of God and to ponder its meaning in our lives. We come together as the people of God to participate in the drama of the unfolding of God's love revealed in the breaking of the one bread and the drinking of the one cup. We come together in the Eucharist to express our common faith in the death and resurrection of Jesus as the source and foundation of the Christian life.

We must see the connection between the table of our homes and the table of the church. When we bring the family gathered at home to gather anew around the table of the Lord, we allow ourselves to be transformed into the body of Christ. Like Christ, we must share what we have received by going forth into the world to preach the Gospel and serve the needs of all.

**Ponder:** How often do I share a meal with my family? How often do I participate in the Eucharist?

**Prayer:** Lord, through your Body and Blood you offer me the gift of eternal life. Help me to make sacrifices and share what I have with the poor.

**Practice:** Today I will invite friends and family to eat together.

# YEAR B

---

*Exodus 24:3–8*
*Psalm 116:12–13, 15–16, 17–18*
*Hebrews 9:11–15*
*Mark 14:12–16, 22–26*

While they were eating, he took a loaf of bread, and after blessing it he broke it, gave it to them, and said, "Take, this is my body." Then he took a cup, and after giving thanks he gave it to them, and all of them drank from it. He said to them, "This is my blood of the covenant, which is poured out for many."

MARK 14:22–24

*Reflection:* The Eucharist teaches us some important lessons for living in the world. When we gather around the table of the Lord, we learn how to live and act like Jesus. In the Eucharist, Jesus teaches us that life is a blessing. No matter what we experience in life, all is a blessing and we need to give thanks to God.

Jesus teaches us in his own life that brokenness is an essential aspect of the Christian life. Unless we are broken, we cannot share in and understand the human condition experienced by many people throughout the world. When we experience the pain of brokenness, we are made vulnerable and are united with the suffering of others. When we recognize that we share in the common weakness of the human condition, we are more likely to pour out love and compassion.

At the heart of the Eucharist is the act of self-giving. The actions of Jesus found in the Eucharist must become our way of acting in the world. The Eucharist becomes a way of life, a countercultural sign against selfishness, greed, the abuse of power, and violence. All who are united in the Eucharist are called to give to others what they have received through the sacrifice of Christ: the love, compassion, and peace of God.

**Ponder:** Why am I afraid to be vulnerable?

**Prayer:** Lord, out of brokenness and weakness you saved my life. Help me to embrace my weakness so that I can walk in solidarity with the poor and suffering.

**Practice:** Today I will be more sensitive to the pain and suffering of the people around me.

# YEAR C

---

*Genesis 14:18–20*
*Psalm 110:1, 2, 3, 4*
*1 Corinthians 11:23–26*
*Luke 9:11b–17*

And taking the five loaves and the two fish, he looked up to heaven, and blessed and broke them, and gave them to the disciples to set before the crowd. And all ate and were filled. What was left over was gathered up, twelve baskets of broken pieces.

LUKE 9:16–17

*Reflection:* We live in a "supersized" culture where we have more than we need. We are accustomed to eating out and often do not consume all the food we order. Perhaps we bring the leftovers home for another meal, but they generally are thrown into the garbage bin. So much food gets wasted while so many people in the world starve to death.

The Eucharist is not just about feeding our spiritual hunger; it is also a call to feed those who lack food and water. We cannot eat at the table of the Lord and not think about our moral duty to feed the poor. We must be aware of the fact that we become the body of Christ by our participation in the Eucharist. We receive from the Eucharist our common mission to feed the hungry, to share with them the love and compassion of God.

The Eucharist challenges us to reassess our lifestyle—especially our food consumption—in light of God's generosity. We need to be more mindful of the ways we waste food and abuse the resources of the earth. In the Eucharist we are called to give to others what Jesus has given to us: food for life. Jesus, who is present with us in the Eucharist, invites us to be more proactive in our efforts to eradicate global poverty.

**Ponder:** How much food do I waste during the week?

**Prayer:** Lord, you love me and answer all my needs. Help me to be less self-focused in life and more attentive to the needs of others.

**Practice:** Today I will be mindful of what I eat and not be wasteful. I will tithe and give to a local charity.

# Ordinary Time

As we step again into Ordinary Time,
let us be intentional about embodying the
Easter gifts of faith, joy, hope, and forgiveness
throughout the liturgical year.

# Tenth Sunday in Ordinary Time

## YEAR A

---

*Hosea 6:3–6*
*Psalm 50:1, 8, 12–13, 14–15*
*Romans 4:18–25*
*Matthew 9:9–13*

**The Pharisees said to his disciples, "Why does your teacher eat with tax collectors and sinners?"**

**MATTHEW 9:11**

*Reflection:* Our perception of the world is conditioned by our limited human experiences. We look at people and judge them through the lens of our racial, cultural, ethnic, religious, political, and socioeconomic backgrounds. Our impressions of others are also created and supported by messages conveyed through the mass media. We feel comfortable in situations where people share our viewpoints, reflect our values, affirm our beliefs, and support our lifestyle.

We do not easily interact with people who have been labeled different, social outcasts, underprivileged, poor, abnormal, or strange. We are not open to welcoming people who might challenge us with another point of view to change our thoughts, ideas, and attitudes. We are afraid to admit that we have been intolerant and prejudiced toward others. We remain stubborn-minded, arrogant, and insensitive toward those who are not like us.

As Christians, our perception of the world and understanding of people must be conditioned by the life and teachings of Jesus. Jesus eats with sinners and outcasts to teach us what it means to be faithful to God's command to love God and neighbor. The sinners and outcasts who come to listen to God's Word teach us what it means to be a faithful disciple. Jesus shows us that the kingdom of God is available to all people and that God's love is universal.

Our love for God and our love for neighbor are inseparable. We cannot love God without loving our neighbor. God's Word changes our hearts and invites us to embrace God's vision for humanity. Faithfulness to God's commands transcends the limitations and prejudices of this world. Our faith compels us to see and love every person as a child of God.

*Ponder:* What prejudices do I harbor in my heart?

*Prayer:* Lord, you teach us to love God and neighbor unconditionally. Help me to be faithful in showing love and respect to all people.

*Practice:* Today I will work on changing my negative thoughts and feelings toward others.

# YEAR B

*Genesis 3:9–15*
*Psalm 130:1–2, 3–4, 5–6, 7–8*
*2 Corinthians 4:13—5:1*
*Mark 3:20–35*

**Looking at those who sat around him, [Jesus] said, "Here are my mother and my brothers! Whoever does the will of God is my brother and sister and mother."**

MARK 3:34–35

***Reflection:*** We become family when we sit down together at table to eat, share stories, and discuss the challenges of life. We build community when we sit down with people to discern a common vision, common goals, common values, and the common good. We learn about the meaning and purpose of life when we sit down together to find concrete ways to address the needs of the poor. We can do good things when people from all walks of life are of one mind and one heart.

We jeopardize our life together when we allow pride and arrogance to become the norm. We increase the chances for conflict, war, and violence when we share nothing in common. We waste the precious gifts of time, energy, talent, and resources when we refuse to sit down together to resolve our differences. We diminish the possibility for reconciliation and peace when we do not listen to the opinions of others. We destroy families and communities when we fail to respect people. We cannot accomplish good things in life when we are not of one mind and one heart.

We come to know the will of God when we sit down together to prayerfully read and meditate on the gospels and learn to live out the teachings of Jesus in our lives. God's will demands that we love and respect one another as brothers and sisters, serve the needs of all, and live in peace together. We can experience heaven on earth when our words and actions are in accordance with the will of God.

**Ponder:** When do I think about the will of God?

**Prayer:** Lord, you reveal to us the will of God. Help me to know and live out the will of God in my life.

**Practice:** Today I will be faithful in doing the will of God.

# YEAR C

———

*1 Kings 17:17–24*
*Psalm 30:2, 4, 5–6, 11, 12, 13*
*Galatians 1:11–19*
*Luke 7:11–17*

For I want you to know, brothers and sisters, that the gospel that was proclaimed by me is not of human origin; for I did not receive it from a human source, nor was I taught it, but I received it through a revelation of Jesus Christ.

GALATIANS 1:11–12

**Reflection:** We learn about life from interacting with our parents, teachers, friends, colleagues, coworkers, and many other people we encounter in various situations. We trust that certain people will share with us not only their personal experiences but also good, reliable information to help us live good, healthy, and productive lives. We receive insights into the human condition through our relationships with others.

We learn how to perform certain tasks by working with gifted and talented people. We learn how to play a musical instrument by working with an experienced musician. We learn how to cook by working with a trained chef. We learn how to act by working with an actor. We learn how to build houses by working with a skilled carpenter. Whatever we have learned in life can be traced back to an experience with an individual or a group of people whom we have trusted and respected.

We need people who have a relationship with Jesus and who are committed to reading the Scriptures to show us how to experience the love and compassion of God. We need people who have been touched by the mercy and forgiveness of God to teach us to forgive others. We need people who are not afraid to share their faith in God to lead us to a change of heart. Whatever we learn about God can be traced to God's Spirit working through the hearts and lives of believers.

*Ponder:* What is the source of my faith in God?

*Prayer:* Lord, you are the revelation of God's love and compassion in the world. Help me to be a witness of your love and compassion to others.

*Practice:* Today I will be an example of God's love and compassion.

# Monday of the Tenth Week in Ordinary Time

## YEAR I

*2 Corinthians 1:1–7*
*Psalm 34:2–3, 4–5, 6–7, 8–9*

## YEAR II

*1 Kings 17:1–6*
*Psalm 121:1bc–2, 3–4, 5–6, 7–8*

## YEARS I AND II

*Matthew 5:1–12*

**Jesus taught them, saying, "Blessed are the pure in heart, for they will see God."**

MATTHEW 5:1, 8

*Reflection:* Faith opens our eyes to see God in our brothers and sisters. Faith opens our ears to hear the voice of God in unexpected places. Faith widens, deepens, and extends our capacity for love, compassion, and forgiveness. Faith hones our attention so that we are focused on the things of God. Faith purifies our hearts to trust in God's personal love for us and to rely on the power of love and peace to transform the world. Faith blesses our lives with meaning and purpose, and we in turn bless the lives of others with the purity of our faith in God's love and mercy.

To have the assurance of Jesus' blessings as we wake up each day keeps our faith fresh and helps us to choose the way of compassion and reconciliation in our daily encounters with family, friends, coworkers, and even strangers. Sometimes we struggle to remain pure in our intention to live faith-filled lives. In these times, we need to take a few precious minutes to reconnect with God in our hearts. We need to set aside time to read holy Scripture and be inspired once again by God's Word of love. We need to remain aware of every opportunity to ask for God's help and guidance. We need to spend moments in prayer, asking God to show us God's will for us.

Blessed are we as we come to know, love, and serve God, the One who loves us unconditionally, walks with us in every moment, and helps us to grow in faith, hope, and purity.

*Ponder:* What blessings do I bring to the world?

*Prayer:* Lord, your love heals our brokenness. Purify me that my faith in your love and compassion may touch the lives of the brokenhearted.

*Practice:* Today I will have faith in God's love for me.

# Tuesday of the
# Tenth Week in Ordinary Time

## YEAR I

*2 Corinthians 1:18–22*
*Psalm 119:129, 130, 131, 132, 133, 135*

## YEAR II

*1 Kings 17:7–16*
*Psalm 4:2–3, 4–5, 7b–8*

## YEARS I AND II

*Matthew 5:13–16*

**Jesus taught them, saying, "You are the salt of the earth; but if salt has lost its taste, how can its saltiness be restored?"**

**MATTHEW 5:13**

*Reflection:* Jesus reminds us of our inner goodness and love: We are the salt of the earth; we give flavor to life by our presence and by sharing our goodness, kindness, and compassion in the world. No one else has the same flavor we do; we each have our unique gifts, talents, and creativity. Jesus wants us to know that we are valuable human persons. Our lives have meaning and purpose.

Jesus also reminds us that, in our humanness, we often become tired, discouraged, fretful, and isolated. We lose our zest for life. We doubt our abilities. We feel crushed by others' demands. We seek approval from others to feel good about ourselves. We worry about finances, health, and responsibilities. We keep busy taking care of others and neglect our own needs.

When we become aware that our lives lack meaning, we need to turn to God. We need to offer our weakness, our frailty, and our discouragement to God and ask for healing. We need to spend quiet time in prayer, listening for God's direction. We need to deepen our relationship with Jesus by reading and reflecting on sacred Scripture. We need to open our hearts to the truth that we are precious, magnificent beings created in the likeness of God's love and goodness. We need to thank God for the gift of life and ask to be shown how we can use our own particular talents and gifts to make the world thirsty for the kingdom of God.

**Ponder:** How am I the salt of the earth?

**Prayer:** Lord, you hear me when I call on you. Grant me the faith to turn to you when my life seems empty and lacking in meaning.

**Practice:** Today I will use my gifts and talents to help someone in need.

# Wednesday of the Tenth Week in Ordinary Time

## YEAR I

*2 Corinthians 3:4–11*
*Psalm 99:5, 6, 7, 8, 9*

## YEAR II

*1 Kings 18:20–39*
*Psalm 16:1b–2ab, 4, 5ab and 8, 11*

## YEARS I AND II

*Matthew 5:17–19*

**Jesus taught them, saying, "Do not think that I have come to abolish the law or the prophets; I have come not to abolish but to fulfill."**

MATTHEW 5:17

*Reflection:* The law Jesus came to fulfill is the law of love: love of God, love of self, and love of neighbor. Jesus fulfills the law of love by healing those who are blind, deaf, and lame. He fulfills the law of love by welcoming the rejected and abandoned, eating with sinners, and socializing with those considered outcasts. He fulfills the law of love by washing the feet of the disciples, teaching the people, and preaching God's way of mercy, forgiveness, and compassion.

We are called to follow Jesus. We are called to fulfill the law of love. We are called to be mindful of the needs of the poor, of the homeless, of those struggling to make ends meet, of those experiencing hardship, illness, loneliness, and discouragement. We are called to set aside our preconceived notions, our prejudices, our tendency to blame and be afraid. We are called to love all people unconditionally—including ourselves, our families, our friends, those we know, those we don't know, and all those we find difficult to love.

We fulfill the law of love one moment at a time. In every situation we have a choice to love or not to love. Because we are human, sometimes we fail to choose love. Yet our failures become fewer the more we intentionally practice the law of love. Over time we become aware that we are making progress in fulfilling God's law of love, and we realize that only love fulfills us.

*Ponder:* How do I fulfill the law of love?

*Prayer:* Lord, you are our hope. Give me the faith to follow your way of love, peace, and compassion.

*Practice:* Today I will intentionally choose to practice God's love.

# Thursday of the
# Tenth Week in Ordinary Time

## YEAR I

*2 Corinthians 3:15—4:1, 3–6*
*Psalm 85:9ab and 10, 11–12, 13–14*

## YEAR II

*1 Kings 18:41–46 • Psalm 65:10, 11, 12–13*

## YEARS I AND II

*Matthew 5:20–26*

Jesus taught them, saying, "But I say to you that if you are angry with a brother or sister, you will be liable to judgment; and if you insult a brother or sister, you will be liable to the council; and if you say, 'You fool,' you will be liable to the hell of fire."

**MATTHEW 5:22**

***Reflection:*** When we're out driving and someone cuts us off, we might yell "You fool!" automatically, not giving a thought to what we're saying. We are not mindful of how we're really feeling: afraid of being hurt, angry at being disrespected, saddened by someone's inattention to our rights and needs. Despite our venting, our true feelings may go unnamed and unprocessed, continuing to cause us distress. Placing blame for our emotional state on someone else can become an unhealthy habit.

When we insult or address others disrespectfully, we add to the violence that already permeates our world. It's human to feel anger at injustice, anger at abuse, anger at the harsh realities of cruelty, greed, and indifference. Yet when we turn the anger we feel against others, we add to the unrest, dissatisfaction, and lack of accountability that present obstacles to the healing power of God's love. If we could instead be mindful of the anger, acknowledging it as our personal emotional state, we could use its energy to make positive changes to our situation.

Staying mindful in moments of great emotional stress is the work of a lifetime. Yet with every moment of awareness comes the option to choose accountability over blame, harmony over conflict, peace over turmoil. With every moment of awareness comes the faith to spread the good news of reconciliation, forgiveness, and love.

**Ponder:** When have I made others the target of my anger?

**Prayer:** Lord, you are love. Grant me the gift of awareness that my words, actions, and attitudes may reflect your way of peace and harmony.

**Practice:** Today I will reconcile with someone against whom I have been nursing anger.

# Friday of the Tenth Week in Ordinary Time

## YEAR I

*2 Corinthians 4:7–15*
*Psalm 116:10–11, 15–16, 17–18*

## YEAR II

*1 Kings 19:9a, 11–16*
*Psalm 27:7–8a, 8b–9abc, 13–14*

## YEARS I AND II

*Matthew 5:27–32*

Jesus taught them, saying, "You have heard that it was said, 'You shall not commit adultery.' But I say to you that everyone who looks at a woman with lust has already committed adultery with her in his heart."

**MATTHEW 5:27–28**

***Reflection:*** Avoiding the act of adultery is not the fulfillment of the law; avoiding the objectification of others is the fulfillment of the law. When we learn to see one another as living icons of God's love and goodness and make one another the subject of unconditional love and respect, then we are fulfilling the law.

When we forget to look at others with the eyes of love, we become separated from our own heart of goodness. We have lost the sense of our own closeness to God. When we are centered in God, we are serene and compassionate. We have energy to listen to others, to encourage others, to share our faith and conviction in the power of God's love and healing. We live with joy and seek ways to help those in need. We live mindfully, aware of the moment, satisfied with what today has to offer. We don't dwell on the past, harbor grievances, or worry about the future. We have no need to take anything from others, control how others live, or judge others' lifestyles.

When we are living in the heart space of God, we do not objectify others. We understand that no one wants to be the victim of lust, greed, or violence. We acknowledge that we all need God's mercy, forgiveness, compassion, and love. We welcome others as our sisters and brothers and offer everyone the respect due a precious child of God.

**Ponder:** When have I objectified others?

**Prayer:** Hear, O Lord, the sound of my call. Take away whatever prevents me from looking at my sisters and brothers with the eyes of unconditional love.

**Practice:** Today I will make a donation to an organization that protects women and girls from human traffickers.

# Saturday of the
# Tenth Week in Ordinary Time

## YEAR I

*2 Corinthians 5:14–21*
*Psalm 103:1–2, 3–4, 9–10, 11–12*

## YEAR II

*1 Kings 19:19–21*
*Psalm 16:1b–2a and 5, 7–8, 9–10*

## YEARS I AND II

*Matthew 5:33–37*

**Jesus taught them, saying, "And do not swear by your head, for you cannot make one hair white or black."**

**MATTHEW 5:36**

*Reflection:* We like to be in control. We like to organize our time, our lives, and our family's lives. We schedule play dates, appointments, pick-up times, vacations, and family dinners. We send out "save the date" reminders so that others will add our important events to their tight schedules. We like to know where we'll be, where our loved ones will be, how we'll get there, who else will be there, why we're going, what we'll do when we get there, and how it will all unfold.

Jesus reminds us that life is not about being in control but about being aligned with the will of God. God's will is that we love God with our whole heart, mind, and soul, and our neighbors as ourselves. Nothing we do can change God's love for us. Nothing we do can change the truth that each and every member of the human family is a beloved, favored child of God, worthy of respect and dignity.

Our experiences shape our lives. Yet no matter what we have experienced, God is always with us. We need only turn to God in any given moment and ask God to show us what to do and how to do it. We don't need to control events. God will give us everything we need at the right moment.

We do have control over putting our faith in God. Every day we can practice trusting that God is near, that God listens to our prayers, and that God loves us unconditionally and without end.

*Ponder:* What am I trying to control?

*Prayer:* Lord, you abound in kindness. Increase my faith in your loving care for me. Help me to turn my life and will over to you.

*Practice:* Today I will go with the flow instead of planning events for the day.